KU-247-773

The **AA POCKET**Guide

# PARIS

**Original text by Elisabeth Morris**
Updated by Penny Phenix

© Automobile Association Developments Limited 2008
First published 2008
Reprinted July 2008

ISBN: 978-0-7495-5528-3

Published by AA Publishing, a trading name of Automobile Association Developments
Limited, whose registered office is Fanum House, Basing View, Basingstoke, Hampshire
RG21 4EA. Registered number 1878835.

Automobile Association Developments Limited retains the copyright in the original edition
© 1998 and in all subsequent editions, reprints and amendments

A CIP catalogue record for this book is available from the British Library

Colour separation: Keenes, Andover
Printed and bound in Italy by Printer Trento S.r.l.

Front cover images: AA/T Souter
Back cover images: AA/K Paterson

A03876
Maps in this title produced from map data © Tele Atlas N.V. 2005
Transport map © Communicarta Ltd, UK

# About this book

This book is divided into five sections.

**Planning** pages 6–19
Before You Go; Getting There; Getting Around; Being There

**Best places to see** pages 20–41
The unmissable highlights of any visit to Paris

**Exploring** pages 42–97
The best places to visit in Paris, organized by area

**Excursions** pages 98–110
Places to visit out of town

**Maps** pages 115–128
All map references are to the atlas section. For example, Notre-Dame has the reference ➕ 122 C4 – indicating the page number and grid square in which it can be found

# Contents

# Planning

# Before You Go

## WHEN TO GO

| JAN | FEB | MAR | APR | MAY | JUN | JUL | AUG | SEP | OCT | NOV | DEC |
|---|---|---|---|---|---|---|---|---|---|---|---|
| 7°C | 7°C | 10°C | 16°C | 17°C | 23°C | 25°C | 26°C | 21°C | 16°C | 12°C | 8°C |
| 45°F | 45°F | 50°F | 61°F | 63°F | 73°F | 77°F | 79°F | 70°F | 61°F | 54°F | 46°F |

🌧️ 🌧️ 🌧️ ⛅ 🌥️ ☀️ ☀️ ☀️ 🌤️ 🌤️ 🌧️ 🌧️

🔴 High season   ⚪ Low season

Temperatures are the average daily maximum for each month. The best time to visit Paris is June, a glorious month when the days are longest, with the most sunshine and average daytime temperatures a comfortable 23°C (73°F). The city reaches peak tourist capacity in July. August sees the Parisian exodus to the countryside leaving the city emptier than usual. It is the hottest, most humid month and the city is prone to sudden storms. September and October have a high percentage of crisp days and clear skies, but rooms can be difficult to find as this is the peak trade-fair period. Winter temperatures rarely drop below freezing, but it rains frequently, sometimes with hail, from November to January.

## WHAT YOU NEED

● Required
○ Suggested
▲ Not required

Some countries require a passport to remain valid for a minimum period (usually at least six months) beyond the date of entry – check before you travel.

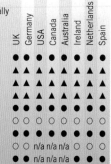

| | UK | Germany | USA | Canada | Australia | Ireland | Netherlands | Spain |
|---|---|---|---|---|---|---|---|---|
| Passport (or National Identity Card where applicable) | ● | ● | ● | ● | ● | ● | ● | ● |
| Visa (regulations can change – check before you travel) | ▲ | ▲ | ▲ | ▲ | ▲ | ▲ | ▲ | ▲ |
| Onward or Return Ticket | ▲ | ▲ | ▲ | ▲ | ▲ | ▲ | ▲ | ▲ |
| Health Inoculations (tetanus and polio) | ▲ | ▲ | ▲ | ▲ | ▲ | ▲ | ▲ | ▲ |
| Health Documentation (▶ 9, Health) | ● | ● | ● | ▲ | ▲ | ● | ● | ● |
| Travel Insurance | ○ | ○ | ○ | ○ | ○ | ○ | ○ | ○ |
| Driving Licence (national) | ● | ● | ● | ● | ● | ● | ● | ● |
| Car Insurance Certificate | ○ | ○ | n/a | n/a | n/a | ○ | ○ | ○ |
| Car Registration Document | ● | ● | n/a | n/a | n/a | ● | ● | ● |

## ADVANCE PLANNING WEBSITES
● Paris Tourist Office: **www.**parisinfo.com (this site also has information for visitors with disabilities)
● Paris Tourisme: **www.**paris-tourism.com
● French Tourist Office: **www.**franceguide.com

## TOURIST OFFICES AT HOME
**In the UK** French Government Tourist Office ✉ 178 Piccadilly, London W1J 9AL ☎ 09068 244123

**In the USA** French Tourist Office ✉ 444 Madison Avenue, 16th Floor, New York, NY10022 ☎ 514/288-1904
French Government Tourist Office ✉ 9454 Wilshire Boulevard, Suite 715, Beverly Hills, CA90212 ☎ 514/288-1904

**In Australia** French Tourist Office ✉ Level 13, 25 Bligh Street, Sydney, NSW 2000 ☎ (02) 9231 5244

**In Canada** French Tourist Office ✉ 1981 avenue McGill, College Suite 490, Montréal H3A 2W9 ☎ 514/288-2026

## HEALTH ADVICE
**Insurance** Nationals of EU countries can obtain medical treatment at reduced cost in France with the relevant documentation (EHIC – European Health Insurance Card), although private medical insurance is still advised and is essential for all other visitors.

**Dental services** As for general medical treatment (see Insurance, opposite), nationals of EU countries can obtain dental treatment at reduced cost. Around 70 per cent of standard dentists' fees are refunded. However, private medical insurance is advised for all visitors.

## TIME DIFFERENCES

| GMT 12 noon | France 1pm | Spain 1pm | USA (NY) 7am | USA (West Coast) 4am | Sydney 10pm |
|---|---|---|---|---|---|

France is on Central European Time, one hour ahead of Greenwich Mean Time (GMT +1). From late March, when clocks are put forward one hour, until late October, French summer time (GMT +2) operates.

## WHAT'S ON WHEN

The events listed here are liable to change from one year to the next and in the case of major festivals, there is often more than one venue. Dates also vary slightly.

## PARIS

**June** *Festival Chopin:* An annual tribute to the Romantic composer at the Orangerie de Bagatelle in the heart of the Bois de Boulogne.
*Fête de la Musique:* On 21 June, Paris's squares, gardens and streets come alive with hundreds of musicians.
*Festival de Théâtre:* Open-air theatre in English and French in the Jardin de Pré Catelan in the Bois de Boulogne.

**June–July** *Paris Jazz Festival:* Open-air concerts in the Parc Floral de Paris, Bois de Vincennes.
*14 July:* Military parade down the Champs-Elysées, fireworks and popular ball to celebrate National Day.

**July–August** *Fête des Tuileries:* Jardin des Tuileries becomes a fairground (begins end of June).
*Paris, Quartier d'Eté:* Open-air music, plays and dance.

**September** *Biennale Internationale des Antiquaires:* Biennial international antiques display (even years); last two weeks September.
*La Villette Jazz Festival:* Jazz in the Grande Halle and Parc de la Villette.

**October** *Foire Internationale d'Art Contemporain:* Exhibition of contemporary art.
*Mondial de l'Automobile:* International motor-car show every two years (even years).

**December** *Salon Nautique International:* International boat show.

## NATIONAL HOLIDAYS

| JAN | FEB | MAR | APR | MAY | JUN | JUL | AUG | SEP | OCT | NOV | DEC |
|-----|-----|-----|-----|-----|-----|-----|-----|-----|-----|-----|-----|
| 1 | | (1) | (1) | 3(4) | (1) | 1 | 1 | | | 2 | 1 |

| | |
|---|---|
| 1 Jan | New Year's Day |
| Mar/Apr | Easter Sunday and Monday |
| 1 May | May Day |
| May | VE (Victory in Europe) Day |
| 6th Thu after Easter | Ascension Day |
| May/Jun | Whit Sunday and Monday |
| 14 Jul | Bastille Day |
| 15 Aug | Assumption Day |
| 1 Nov | All Saints' Day |
| 11 Nov | Remembrance Day |
| 25 Dec | Christmas Day |

Banks, businesses, museums and most shops (except *boulangeries*) are closed on these days.

## ÎLE-DE-FRANCE

**April–May** *Salon des Antiquaires de Rambouillet:* Antiques fair.

**May–June** *Festival de Saint-Denis:* Symphonic concerts take place in Saint-Denis basilica.
*Fête Médiévale:* Medieval pageant, siege warfare demonstrations, tournaments in Provins.
*Le Mois Moière:* Theatre, music and street entertainment in parts of the city of Versailles.

**June–July** *Festival d'Auvers-sur-Oise:* Singing, piano and chamber music.

**July–August** *Fête des Loges de Saint-Germain-en-Laye:* A fair held in Saint-Germain forest.

**July–September** *Festival de l'Orangerie de Sceaux:* Chamber music festival in parc de Sceaux.

**August** *Fête de la Saint-Louis à Fontainebleau:* An ancient royal tradition celebrated by fireworks at the château.

**September** *Fête du Cheval Fontainebleau:* International gathering of horse lovers.
*Barbizon au temps des peintres:* Recalls 1848–70, when the Forêt de Fontainebleau drew artists to Barbizon.

**September–mid-October** *Festival d'Île-de-France:* Concerts and shows in castles, abbeys and churches throughout the region.

# Getting There

**Ticket prices** tend to be highest in spring and summer (Easter to September). City break packages may offer even more savings if a Saturday night is included. Check with the airlines, travel agents and Internet for best deals and offers.

## BY AIR

Paris has two main airports – Roissy Charles de Gaulle (☎ 01 48 62 22 80) where most international flights arrive, and Orly (☎ 01 45 31 16 20). Numerous carriers operate direct flights from Canada and the US, including American Airlines, Delta and Air Canada. From the UK, British Airways, British Midland and easyJet operate regular services; from Australia, Qantas and Continental are the major carriers. France's national airline, Air France (☎ 0820 820 820 in France; 0870 142 4343 in the UK; 800/237-2747 in the US; www.airfrance.com) has scheduled flights from Britain, mainland Europe and beyond, to both main airports. Approximate flying times to Paris: London (1 hour), Dublin (1.5 hours), New York (8 hours), West Coast USA (12 hours), Vancouver (10 hours), Montréal (7.5 hours), Sydney (23 hours), Auckland (21 hours).

It's 23km (14 miles) from Roissy Charles de Gaulle Airport to the city centre and takes between 35 minutes and 1 hour, depending on public transport used. It's 14km (8.5 miles) from Orly Airport to the city centre and takes between 25 and 45 minutes depending on public transport used.

## BY RAIL

The Eurostar passenger train service (tel: 08705 186186 in Britain; www.eurostar.com) from London Waterloo via the Channel Tunnel to Paris Gare du Nord takes 3 hours. This is probably the easiest way to come to Paris as the train brings you into the heart of the city. There are six major railway stations, each handling traffic to different parts of France and

Europe – Gare de Lyon, Gare du Nord, Gare de l'Est, Gare St-Lazare, Gare d'Austerlitz and Gare Montparnasse. French Railways operates high-speed trains (TGV – *Train à Grande Vitesse*) to Paris from main stations throughout France.

## BY SEA
Ferry companies operate regular services from England and Ireland to France, with rail links to Paris. Crossing time: 35 minutes to 6 hours (England); 14–18 hours (Ireland).

## DRIVING
Driving is on the right.

Speed limits on toll motorways

*(autoroutes)* **130kph/80mph** (**110kph/68mph** when wet). Non-toll motorways and dual carriageways: **110kph/68mph** (**100kph/62mph** when wet). Paris ring road *(périphérique)*: **80kph/50mph**.
Speed limits on country roads: **90kph/56mph** (**80kph/50mph** when wet).
Speed limits on urban roads: **50kph/31mph**.

Seatbelts must be worn in front seats at all times and in rear seats where fitted.

Random breath-testing takes place. Never drive under the influence of alcohol.

Leaded petrol is sold as *essence super* (98 octane). Unleaded is available in two grades: *essence sans plomb* (95 octane) and *essence super sans plomb* (98 octane). Diesel *(Gasoil or Gazole)* is also readily available. In Paris filling stations can be hard to spot, often consisting of little more than a few kerb-side pumps.

If you break down on a motorway *(autoroute)* use the orange-coloured emergency phones (located every 2km/1.2 miles) to contact the breakdown service.

# Getting Around

## PUBLIC TRANSPORT

### INTERNAL FLIGHTS

Air France is the leading domestic airline – information (☎ 08 20 82 08 20). Daily departures from Orly and Roissy/Charles-de-Gaulle airports connect Paris with major French cities/towns in an average flight time of one hour.

### RER

The RER (pronounced 'ehr-oo-ehr') is the fast suburban rail service, which also serves the city centre. There are five lines *(lignes):* A, B, C, D and E and the RER is connected with the métro and SNCF suburban network. Services run 5.30am to midnight, with trains every 12 minutes.

### MÉTRO

Paris's underground with over 300 stations ensures you are never more than 500m (550yds) from a métro stop. Lines are numbered 1 to 14 and are known by the names of the stations at each end. Follow the orange *correspondance* signs to change lines. The métro runs daily 5.30am to 12.30am.

### BUSES

Buses are a good way of seeing Paris (especially route 24), although traffic can be very heavy. Bus stops show the numbers of buses that stop there. Buses run 6.30am to 8.30pm with a reduced service on Sunday and after 8.30pm. Bus tickets are the same as those for the métro.

### BOAT

The Batobus river shuttle (☎ 01 44 11 33 99) that plies the Seine provides an unusual view of Paris. It stops at the Eiffel Tower, Musée d'Orsay, St-Germain-des-Prés, Notre-Dame, Jardin des Plantes, Hôtel de Ville, the Louvre and the Champs-Elysées; Feb–Dec 10–10 (to 7pm in winter).

### TAXIS

Taxis can be hailed if you see one with its roof light on. Taxis are metered with a surcharge for luggage, journeys after 10pm and before 6.30am, and for going from and to stations and airports. Queues can be very long, particularly at railway stations.

## CAR

If your car breaks down in Paris, contact the 24-hour repair service (☎ 01 45 31 16 20).

## CAR RENTAL

Car-rental companies have desks at Roissy/Charles-de-Gaulle and Orly airports, and in Paris itself. Car rental is expensive, but airlines and tour operators offer fly-drive, and French Railways (SNCF) have train/car, packages that are cheaper than renting locally.

## ARRONDISSEMENTS

Paris is divided into 20 districts or *arrondissements*, which spiral clockwise from the city centre. The central *arrondissements* are numbered from 1 to 8:

**1** (75001): heart of the Right Bank, centred on the Louvre and the Île de la Cité.

**2** (75002): the commercial district around the Opéra.

**3** and **4** (75003 and 75004): the Marais district and the Île St-Louis.

**5** (75005): the Latin Quarter and the Left Bank.

**6** (75006): the St-Germain district.

**7** (75007): residential Faubourg St-Germain and the Tour Eiffel.

**8** (75008): the chic district of broad avenues radiating out from the Arc de Triomphe.

## CONCESSIONS

**Students/youths** Holders of an International Student Identity Card (ISIC) are entitled to half-price admission to museums and sights and discounted air and ferry tickets, plus inexpensive meals in some student cafeterias. Those under 26, but not a student, with the International Youth Travel Card (or GO 25 Card) qualify for similar discounts as ISIC holders.

**Senior citizens** Visitors aged over 60 can get discounts (up to 50 per cent) in museums, on public transport and in places of entertainment. Discounts apply to holders of the Carte Senior, which can be purchased from the Abonnement (ticket) office of any main railway station. Without the card, show your passport and you may still get the discount.

# Being There

## TOURIST OFFICES

### HEAD OFFICE
● Office de Tourisme de Paris (Paris Tourism Bureau), 25 rue des Pyramides, 75001 Paris, ☎ 08 92 68 30 00 (omit the initial 0 when calling from outside France) **www.**paris-touristoffice.com

### BRANCHES IN PARIS
● Opéra-Grands Magasins 🌐 Mon–Sat 9am–6.30pm
● Gare de Lyon 🌐 Mon–Sat 8am–6pm
● Gare du Nord 🌐 Daily 8am–6pm
● Montmartre (21 place du Tertre) 🌐 Daily 10am–7pm

● Tour Eiffel (Eiffel Tower) 🌐 Late Mar–Oct: daily 11am–6.40pm

### PARIS ÎLE-DE-FRANCE
● Carrousel du Louvre (lower level), ☎ 01 44 50 19 98/08 26 16 66 66 **www.**pidf.com 🌐 Daily 10am–7pm
● Disneyland Resort Paris, place des Passagers-du-Vent, Marne-la-Vallée, 77705, ☎ 01 60 43 33 33
🚇 RER line A, Marne-la-Vallée–Parc Disneyland

## EMBASSIES AND CONSULATES
**UK** ☎ 01 44 51 31 00
**Germany** ☎ 01 53 83 45 00
**USA** ☎ 01 43 12 22 22
**Netherlands** ☎ 01 40 62 33 00
**Spain** ☎ 01 44 43 18 00

## TELEPHONES
All telephone numbers in France comprise 10 digits. Paris and Île de France numbers all begin with 01. There are no area codes, simply dial the number. Most public phones use a phone-card *(télécarte)* sold in units of 50 or 120 from France Telecom shops, post offices, tobacconists and railway stations. Cafés have phones that take coins. Cheap rates generally apply Mon–Fri 7pm–8am, Sat–Sun all day.

## OPENING HOURS

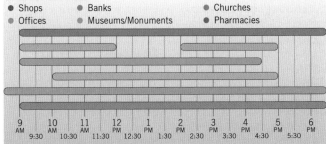

- Shops
- Offices
- Banks
- Museums/Monuments
- Churches
- Pharmacies

In addition to the times shown above, some shops close between noon and 2pm and all day Sunday and Monday. Large department stores open from 9.30am to 6.30pm and until 9 or 10pm one or two days a week. Food shops open 7am to 1.30pm and 4.30 to 8pm; some open Sunday until noon.

Some banks have extended hours, including Saturday morning but most close weekends. Museum and monument opening times vary, but national museums close Tuesday (except the Trianon Palace, the Musée d'Orsay and Versailles which close Monday), while other museums usually close Monday.

### EMERGENCY TELEPHONE NUMBERS
**Police** 17
**Fire** 18
**Ambulance** 15
**Doctor** (24-hour call out) 01 47 07 77 77

### INTERNATIONAL DIALLING CODES
Dial 00 followed by:
**UK:** 44
**Ireland:** 353
**USA/Canada:** 1
**Australia:** 61

**Germany:** 49
**Spain:** 34

### POSTAL SERVICES
Post offices are identified by a yellow or brown 'La Poste' or 'PTT' sign. The main office at 52 rue du Louvre is open 24 hours. The branch at 71 avenue des Champs-Elysées is open Mon–Fri 9am–7.30pm, Sat 10am–7pm.

### ELECTRICITY
The power supply in Paris is 220 volts. Sockets accept two-round-pin

(or increasingly three-round-pin) plugs, so an adaptor is needed for most non-Continental appliances. A transformer is needed for appliances operating on 110–120 volts.

## CURRENCY AND EXCHANGE

**Currency** The French unit of currency is the euro (€). Coins are issued in denominations of 1, 2, 5, 10, 20 and 50 cents and €1 and €2. There are 100 cents in €1. Notes (bills) are issued in denominations of €5, €10, €20, €50, €100, €200 and €500.

**Exchange** You can exchange travellers' cheques at some banks and at bureaux de change at airports, main railway stations or in some department stores, and exchange booths. All transactions are subject to a hefty commission charge, so you may prefer to rely on cash and credit cards. Travellers'

cheques issued by American Express and Visa can also be changed at many post offices.

**Credit cards** are widely accepted in shops, restaurants and hotels. Visa, MasterCard and Diners Club cards with four-digit PINs can be used in most ATMs.

## HEALTH AND SAFETY

**Sun advice** July and August (when most Parisians leave the city) are the sunniest (and hottest) months. If 'doing the sights' cover up or apply a sunscreen and take plenty of fluids.

**Drugs** Pharmacies – recognized by their green cross sign – have highly qualified staff who are able to offer medical advice, provide first aid and prescribe a wide range of drugs, though some are available by prescription *(ordonnance)* only.

## TIPS/GRATUITIES

Yes ✓   No ✗

| | | |
|---|---|---|
| Hotels (service included) | ✓ | change |
| Restaurants (service included) | ✓ | change |
| Cafés/bars (service included) | ✓ | change |
| Taxis | ✓ | €1 |
| Tour guides | ✓ | €1 |
| Porters | ✓ | €1 |
| Hairdressers | ✓ | €1 |
| Cloakroom attendants | ✓ | 15–30c |
| Theatre/cinema usherettes | ✓ | 30c |
| Toilets | ✓ | change |

**Safe water** It is quite safe to drink tap water in Paris and all over France, but never drink from a tap marked *eau non potable* (not drinking water). Mineral water is fairly cheap and widely available.

**Petty crime,** particularly theft of wallets and handbags is fairly common in Paris. Be aware of innocent, scruffy-looking children – they may be working the streets in gangs, fleecing tourists. Report loss or theft to the Police Municipale (blue uniforms). To be safe:
● Watch your bag on the métro, in areas like the Champs-Elysées and Beaubourg and in museum queues.
● Cars should be well-secured.
● Put valuables in your hotel safe.

## PHOTOGRAPHY

**What to photograph:** Paris's monumental buildings and animated Parisians drinking in pavement cafés.

**Where you need permission to photograph:** certain museums will allow you to photograph inside. In churches with mural paintings and icons where flashlight is required, ask permission first.

**Where to buy film:** shops and photo laboratories sell the most popular brands and types of film. Rapid film development is possible but quite expensive.

## CLOTHING SIZES

| France | UK | Rest of Europe | USA | |
|---|---|---|---|---|
| 46 | 36 | 46 | 36 | |
| 48 | 38 | 48 | 38 | |
| 50 | 40 | 50 | 40 | |
| 52 | 42 | 52 | 42 | |
| 54 | 44 | 54 | 44 | **Suits** |
| 56 | 46 | 56 | 46 | |
| 41 | 7 | 41 | 8 | |
| 42 | 7.5 | 42 | 8.5 | |
| 43 | 8.5 | 43 | 9.5 | |
| 44 | 9.5 | 44 | 10.5 | |
| 45 | 10.5 | 45 | 11.5 | **Shoes** |
| 46 | 11 | 46 | 12 | |
| 37 | 14.5 | 37 | 14.5 | |
| 38 | 15 | 38 | 15 | |
| 39/40 | 15.5 | 39/40 | 15.5 | |
| 41 | 16 | 41 | 16 | |
| 42 | 16.5 | 42 | 16.5 | **Shirts** |
| 43 | 17 | 43 | 17 | |
| 36 | 8 | 34 | 6 | |
| 38 | 10 | 36 | 8 | |
| 40 | 12 | 38 | 10 | |
| 42 | 14 | 40 | 12 | |
| 44 | 16 | 42 | 14 | **Dresses** |
| 46 | 18 | 44 | 16 | |
| 38 | 4.5 | 38 | 6 | |
| 38 | 5 | 38 | 6.5 | |
| 39 | 5.5 | 39 | 7 | |
| 39 | 6 | 39 | 7.5 | |
| 40 | 6.5 | 40 | 8 | **Shoes** |
| 41 | 7 | 41 | 8.5 | |

# Best
places
to see

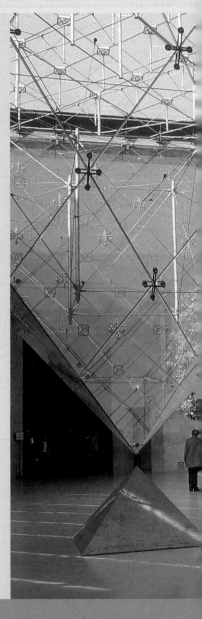

1

# Centre Georges Pompidou

**www.**centrepompidou.fr

**This spacious and convivial art centre, in the heart of historic Paris, houses under one roof all forms of modern and contemporary art.**

With 25,000 visitors a day, the Centre Georges Pompidou is now one of Paris's top sights. Yet at the time it was built, close to the historic Marais which is famous for its elegant architecture, the 'refinery', as Rogers and Piano's post-modern building was nicknamed, deeply shocked French people. In fact, the revolutionary concept of this

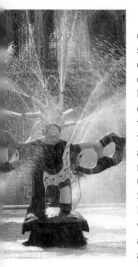

open-plan 'house of culture for all' ensured its success and brought life back to the district. The centre has had its first major face-lift and been completely refurbished inside; its main asset, the Musée National d'Art Moderne, reached by the external escalator, gained extra exhibition space in the process. The museum is dedicated to the main trends of art from 1905 to the present day. Modern art is displayed on level 5. Particularly well represented are Fauvism (Dufy, Derain, Matisse), Cubism (Braque, Picasso, Léger), Dadaism, Surrealism (Dali, Miró), Expressionism (Soutine, Kirchner, Modigliani and to a lesser extent Chagall), various forms of abstract art (Kandinsky, Klee, but also Poliakoff, Dubuffet and the CoBrA movement), and pre-1960 American painting. The collections of contemporary art (level 4) include exponents of the new realism (Arman, César), of Pop Art (Warhol), of Minimalist art (Sol Lewitt, Buren) and of monochromes (Manzoni, Klein).

The centre also houses a library, the Institute for Acoustic and Musical Research, the Centre for Industrial Creation, a large exhibition hall, a children's workshop and a reconstruction of Brancusi's workshop.

➕ 123 A5 ✉ Place Georges-Pompidou, 75004 ☎ 01 44 78 12 33 🕐 Centre: Wed–Mon. Modern art museum and exhibitions: 11–9. Library: weekdays 12–10; weekends 11–10. Brancusi workshop 2–6 🏷 Free access; museum: moderate (includes Brancusi workshop, children's workshop and level 6) 🍽 Restaurant (€€), café and snack bar 🚇 Rambuteau, Hôtel de Ville 🚌 38, 47, 75 ❓ Audioguides, ATM, shops

# 2 Les Champs-Elysées

**www.**monum.fr

AVENUE
des
CHAMPS ELYSEES
8eme

**For most visitors this prestigious avenue epitomizes French elegance, but it is also a dazzling place of entertainment and a luxury shopping mall.**

In the late 17th century, André Le Nôtre designed a gently rising alleyway as an extension of the Jardin des Tuileries. This later lost its rustic appearance and became a fashionable avenue lined with elegant restaurants and cafés. Nowadays it is the traditional venue for a variety of events such as the Paris Marathon, the arrival of the Tour de France and the march past on 14 July, which celebrates France's national day. But 'les Champs' (the fields) is also a place where people of all ages just relax and feel alive.

The lower section, stretching from the place de la Concorde (with breathtaking views along the whole length of the avenue) to the Rond-Point des Champs-Elysées, is laid out as an English-style park shaded by imposing chestnut trees. On the left are the Grand and Petit Palais, two temples of the arts, while on the right is a monument to the French Resistance hero, Jean Moulin, who was reburied in the Panthéon on 19 December 1964.

The upper section stretches from the Rond-Point, designed by Le Nôtre, to the Arc de Triomphe. This is the 'modern'

part of the avenue, with its pavements now revamped and restored to their former comfortable width. Banks, cinemas, airline offices, car showrooms and large cafés spread out on the pavements, lining the way to the place de l'Etoile. Fashion boutiques cluster along the arcades running between the Champs-Elysées and the parallel rue de Ponthieu. Some shops remain open well into the night and the bustle only quietens down in the early hours of the morning.

✚ 117 E5 ✉ Avenue des Champs Elysées, 75008
🍴 Choice of restaurants (€–€€€) Ⓜ Concorde, Champs-Elysées-Clemenceau, Franklin-D Roosevelt, George V, Charles-de-Gaulle-Etoile 🚌 32, 42, 73

# 3 La Grande Arche de la Défense

**www.**grandearche.com

**Symbolically guarding the western approach to the city, the Grande Arche is both a recognition of tradition and a bold step towards the future.**

From the arch's roof top (110m/360ft above ground), accessible by the exterior lift, a marvellous view unfolds in a straight line along an axis to the Arc de Triomphe and, beyond, to the Obelisk at place de la Concorde and to the Louvre, extending the magnificent vista opened up by Le Nôtre. The arch was inaugurated in 1989 for the bicentenary celebrations of the French Revolution and is now a major tourist attraction. The stark simplicity of its architectural outline and the materials used are definitely contemporary, while its sheer size is a marvel of modern technology. The Danish architect, Otto von Spreckelsen, built a perfect hollow concrete cube covered over with glass and white

Carrara marble. Steps lead up to the central platform, where the lifts are to be found.

The arch dominates a vast square, known as Le Parvis, decorated with colourful sculptures, including a red 'stabile' by Calde, and flanked by another remarkable building: the CNIT (Centre of New Industries and Technology), shaped like an upside-down-shell, which serves mainly as a conference centre but is also a pleasant meeting place for business people. There are several cafés and a branch of the FNAC, the French equivalent of Virgin stores, stocking a large selection of CDs covering a wide spectrum of musical tastes.

Opposite, there is a huge shopping centre known as Les Quatre Temps, which has some of the best shopping bargains in Paris. Its focal point is the vast hypermarket Auchan.

🔖 116 C1 (off map) ✉ 1 parvis de la Défense, 92044 Paris-La Défense ☎ 01 49 07 27 57 (Grande Arche) 🕐 Grande Arche: daily 10–7 🛗 Lift (elevator) of Grande Arche: moderate 🍴 Rooftop restaurant, snackbars and cafés in Les Quatre Temps shopping centre (€) and in the CNIT (€ and €€) 🚇 La Défense 🚌 73, Balabus in summer ❓ Video presentation, guided tours, shops

# 4 Les Invalides

**www.**invalides.org

**This is one of Paris's most imposing architectural ensembles, built around two churches and housing several museums.**

The Hôtel National des Invalides was commissioned by Louis XIV as a home for wounded soldiers. It is a splendid example of 17th-century architecture, the classical austerity of its 200m-long (656ft) façade being offset by the baroque features of the Église du Dôme, with its gilt dome glittering above the slate roofs of the stone buildings. The huge esplanade filling the gap between the river and the monumental entrance enhances the majesty of the building.

The museums are accessible from the arcaded main courtyard. The Musée de l'Armée is one of the richest museums of its kind in the world. It contains weapons from all over the world, armour and uniforms, mementoes of famous generals, paintings, documents and models. Particularly striking is the comprehensive permanent exhibition devoted to World War II.

The Musée des Plans-Reliefs is a fascinating collection of models of fortified French towns, originally started at Louis XIV's request.

On the far side of the courtyard is the entrance to St-Louis-des-Invalides, the soldiers' church, which contains a colourful collection of flags brought back from various campaigns.

The magnificent Église du Dôme, built by Jules Hardouin-Mansart, is a striking contrast: an elegant façade with two tiers of Doric and Corinthian columns and an imposing gilt dome surmounted by a slender lantern. The splendid interior decoration is enhanced by the marble floor. The open circular crypt houses Napoleon's red porphyry tomb.

🕂 121 B4 ✉ Esplanade des Invalides, 75007 ☎ 01 44 42 37 72 🕐 6 Apr to mid-Jun and late Sep daily 10–5; mid-Jun to mid-Sep daily 10–7. Closed 1 Jan, 1 May, 1 Nov, 25 Dec 🎫 Moderate 🍴 Restaurant (€) 🚇 Invalides, La Tour Maubourg, Varenne 🚌 28, 63, 69, 80, 82, 84, 87, 92, 93 ❓ Audiovisual shows, guided tours, shops

# 5 Le Louvre

**www.**louvre.fr

**This former royal palace, which celebrated its bicentenary in 1993, is today one of the largest museums in the world.**

## THE PALACE

Excavations carried out in 1977 under the Cour Carrée, the courtyard surrounded by the oldest part of the palace, led to the discovery of the original castle built around 1200 by King Philippe-Auguste. The tour of the foundations of this medieval Louvre, including the base of the keep, the moat and the outer wall, starts from the main entrance hall under the glass pyramid.

The first palace, built by Pierre Lescot in the style of the Italian Renaissance, was enlarged round the Cour Carrée and along the Seine during the following 200 years. Louis XIV enclosed the Cour Carrée with the stately colonnade that faces the Church of St-Germain-l'Auxerrois. Soon afterwards, however, the King left for Versailles and the palace was neglected by the royal family and the court.

Building was resumed by Napoleon, who built part of the north wing and erected the exquisite Arc de Triomphe du Carrousel. During the second half of the 19th century, Napoleon III completed the Louvre along its rue de Rivoli side.

## THE MUSEUM

The collections are divided into eight departments:
● Egyptian Antiquities include a pink granite *Sphinx from Tanis*, a huge *head of Amenophis IV-Akhenaten* and the famous *Seated Scribe*.

- The most remarkable exhibits in the Oriental Antiquities Department must be the *Assyrian winged bulls*.
- The Greek, Etruscan and Roman Antiquities department contains many masterpieces: don't miss the *Vénus de Milo*, *Winged Victory* and Graeco-Roman sculpture in the Salle des Cariatides.
- The painting collections comprise a fine selection from the Italian school (Fra Angelico, Leonardo da Vinci, Giotto, Veronese, Titian, Raphael), the French school (Poussin, Watteau, Georges de la Tour), the Dutch school (Rembrandt, Rubens, Vermeer) and Spanish masters (Murillo, Goya and El Greco).
- French sculpture is well represented and includes works by Goujon, Houdon and Pradier.
- Objets d'art, displayed to full advantage in the Richelieu wing, include beautiful tapestries and historic items such as Charlemagne's sword.
- The department of Graphic Art houses drawings, prints and watercolours.
- The department of Islamic Art is housed in a new exhibition space in the Cour Visconti.

🔢 122 A2 ✉ 99 rue de Rivoli, 75001. Main entrance via pyramid ☎ Recorded info: 01 40 20 51 51; reception desk: 01 40 20 53 17; visitors with disabilities: 01 40 20 59 90 🕐 Thu–Sun 9–6, Mon and Wed 9am–9.45pm. Closed 1 Jan, 1 May, 11 Nov, 25 Dec ✋ Moderate until 3pm, reduced fee after 3 and Sun, free on 1st Sun of month. To avoid a long wait, buy your ticket in advance online 🍴 Restaurants (€ and €€) and cafés below pyramid and in Carrousel du Louvre 🚇 Palais-Royal/Musée du Louvre 🚌 21, 24, 27. 39, 48, 68, 69, 72, 81, 95 ❓ Guided tours, lectures, concerts, film shows, shops

# 6 Notre-Dame

**www.**cathedraldeparis.com

**This masterpiece of Gothic architecture is one of Paris's most famous landmarks and one of France's most visited religious monuments.**

In 1163, the Bishop of Paris, Maurice de Sully, launched the building of the cathedral, which took nearly 200 years to complete. One of the architects involved was Pierre de Montreuil, who also built the nearby Sainte-Chapelle (► 53). Later alterations deprived the church of its rood screen and of some of its original stained glass; its statues were mutilated during the Revolution because the Commune thought they were likenesses of the kings of France; the cathedral also lost all its original bells, except the *'gros bourdon'*, known as Emmanuel, which is traditionally heard on occasions of national importance. Restoration work was carried out in the 19th century by the famous architect Viollet-le-Duc and the area round the cathedral was cleared.

From across the vast square in front of the cathedral you can admire the harmonious proportions and almost perfect symmetry of the façade. The richly decorated portals are surmounted by statues of the kings of Judaea, restored by Viollet-le-Duc. Above the central rose window, a colonnade links the elegant twin towers; there is a splendid view from the south tower, if you can face up to the 387-step climb.

The nave is 130m (426ft) long, 48m (157ft) wide and 35m (115ft) high; the side chapels are

richly decorated with paintings, sculptures and funeral monuments. Note the beautiful rose window at each end of the transept. The former vestry, on the right of the chancel, houses the Cathedral Treasure, which includes a piece of the Holy Cross.

✚ 122 C4 ✉ Place du Parvis de Notre-Dame, 75004 ☎ 01 42 34 56 10 🕐 Cathedral: daily 8–6.45; closed some religious feast days. Treasure: Mon–Sat 9.30–11.30, 1–5.30. Towers: Apr–Sep daily 9.30–7.30 (Jul–Aug Sat–Sun 9.30am–11pm); Oct–end Mar daily 10.30–5.30 ✋ Cathedral: free; treasure and towers: inexpensive 🍴 Left Bank (€–€€) 🚇 Cité, Saint-Michel 🚌 21, 24, 27, 38, 47, 85, 96

# 7 Orsay, Musée d'

**www.**musee-orsay.fr

**Once a mainline railway station, the Musée d'Orsay has been successfully converted into one of Paris's three major art museums.**

Built in 1900, the Gare d'Orsay was narrowly saved from demolition by a daring plan to turn it into a museum dedicated to all forms of art from 1848 to 1914, and intended as the chronological link between the Louvre and the Musée National d'Art Moderne. The Musée d'Orsay was inaugurated by President Mitterrand in 1986.

The main hall, with the station clock, was retained to create a sense of unity between painting, sculpture, architecture, design, photography and the cinema. The collections are spread over three levels:

● The Lower Level deals with the years from 1848 to 1880; small flights of steps lead off the central alleyway to various exhibition areas where major sculptures are displayed, including a group of graceful figures by Carpeaux entitled *La Danse*. On either side is a comprehensive collection of

paintings of the same period – works by Ingres, Delacroix, Corot, Courbet and the Realists, as well as the beginning of Impressionism with early works by Monet, Manet, Pissarro and others.

● On the Upper Level is the prestigious Impressionist and post-Impressionist collection, undoubtedly the main attraction of the museum: masterpieces are by Manet *(Olympia)*, Degas *(Blue Dancers)*, Sisley *(Snow in Louveciennes)*, Renoir *(Bathers)*, Monet *(The Houses of Parliament, Rouen Cathedral)*, Cézanne *(The Card Players)*, Van Gogh *(The Church at Auvers-sur-Oise)*, Gauguin and the school of Pont-Aven, Matisse, Toulouse-Lautrec and many others.

● The Middle Level is dedicated to the period from 1870 to 1914 and includes important works by Rodin *(Balzac)*, paintings by the Nabis school, as well as a comprehensive section on art nouveau (Lalique, Gallé, Guimard, Mackintosh and Wright).

✚ 121 A6 ✉ 62 rue de Lille (entrance rue de Légion d'Honneur), 75007 ☎ 01 40 49 48 14; 01 40 49 48 00 🕔 Tue–Sat 10–6, Sun 9–6; late night: Thu 9.45 (opens 9am, Jul–Sep). Closed Mon, 1 Jan, 1 May, 25 Dec ✋ Moderate, free first Sun each month 🍴 Restaurant (€), café (€) 🚇 Solférino 🚌 24, 63, 68, 69, 73, 83, 84, 94 ❓ Guided tours, shops, concerts, film shows

# 8 Les Quais

**Walk along the banks of the Seine between the pont de la Concorde and the pont de Sully for some of Paris's finest views.**

In 1992, the river banks from the pont d'Iéna, where the Tour Eiffel stands, to the pont de Sully, at the tip of the Île Saint-Louis, were added to Unesco's list of World Heritage Sites. Here the townscape has an indefinable charm inspired by the harmonious blend of colours: the pale greys and blues of the water and the sky, the soft green of the trees lining the embankment and the mellow stone colour of the historic buildings. Parisians have been strolling along the embankments for centuries, window-shopping, browsing through the *bouquinistes'* stalls or simply watching the activity on both sides of the river.

## THE RIGHT BANK

Start from the pont du Carrousel and walk up-river past the imposing façade of the Louvre. From the pont Neuf, enjoy a fine view of the Conciergerie on the Île de la Cité, or admire the birds and exotic fish on the quai de la Mégisserie. Continue past the Hôtel de Ville towards the lovely pont Marie leading to the peaceful Île Saint-Louis. Cross over to the Left Bank.

## THE LEFT BANK

The familiar green boxes of the *bouquinistes* are here as well! Admire the stunning views of Notre-Dame and its magnificent flying buttresses. The quai Saint-Michel is a favourite haunt of students looking for second-hand books. Further on, stand on the pont des Arts for a romantic view of the historic heart of Paris before walking past the stately façade of the Musée d'Orsay towards the pont de la Concorde.

✚ 122 C4 ✉ Quai du Louvre, quai de la Mégisserie (75001), quai de Gesvres, quai de l'Hôtel de Ville, quai des Célestins (75004), quai de la Tournelle, quai de Montebello, quai St-Michel (75005), quai des Grands Augustins, quai de Conti, quai Malaquais (75006), quai Voltaire, quai Anatole-France (75007) 🍽 Restaurants and cafés along the way, particularly near place du Châtelet and place de l'Hôtel de Ville on the Right Bank, and around place St-Michel on the Left Bank (€–€€€) 🚇 Pont-Neuf, Châtelet, Hôtel de Ville, Pont-Marie, St-Michel, Solférino 🚌 24 follows the Left Bank ❓ Boat trips along the Seine from pont de l'Alma right round the islands

# 9 La Tour Eiffel

**www.**tour-eiffel.fr

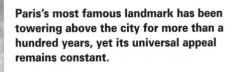

**Paris's most famous landmark has been towering above the city for more than a hundred years, yet its universal appeal remains constant.**

The Tour Eiffel was built by the engineer Gustave Eiffel as a temporary attraction for the 1889 World Exhibition. At the time, its 300m (984ft) height made it the tallest building in the world and an unprecedented technological achievement. It met with instant success, was celebrated by poets and

artists, and its spindly silhouette was soon famous all over the world. In spite of this, it was nearly pulled down when the concession expired in 1909 but was saved because of its invaluable radio aerial, joined in 1957 by television aerials. It was later raised by another 20m (66ft) to accommodate a meteorological station. The iron frame weighs 7,000 tonnes, yet the pressure it exerts on the ground is only 4kg per sq cm; 40 tonnes of paint are used to repaint it every seven years. To celebrate its one hundredth birthday, it was renovated and halogen lighting was installed making it even more spectacular at night.

There are three levels, all accessible by lift, or by stairs – first and second floors only. Information about the tower is available on the first floor (57m/187ft above ground); there are also a restaurant, a gift shop and a post office, where letters are postmarked Paris Tour Eiffel.

The second floor (115m/377ft above ground) offers fine views of Paris, several boutiques and a restaurant appropriately named Jules Verne.

For a spectacular aerial view of the capital go up to the third floor (276m/905ft above ground). There is also a reconstruction of Gustave Eiffel's study and panoramic viewing tables showing 360-degree photos of Paris with the city's landmarks.

✚ 120 A1 ✉ Champ de Mars, 75007 ☎ 01 44 11 23 23 🕐 Jan to mid-Jun and Sep–Dec daily 9.30am–11pm, (stairs to 6); mid-Jun to Aug daily 9am–midnight 🛗 Lift (elevator): 1st–2nd floors inexpensive–moderate, 3rd floor expensive 🍴 Restaurants (€–€€€) 🚇 Bir-Hakeim 🚌 42, 69, 72, 82, 87

# 10 La Villette

**www.**cite-sciences.fr
**www.**cite-musique.fr

**The Cité des Sciences et de l'Industrie and the Cité de la Musique revitalized the outer district of La Villette, turning it into a new cultural centre.**

Situated just inside the boulevard Périphérique, between the Porte de la Villette and the Porte de Pantin, the 30-ha (74-acre) parc de la Villette was laid out on the site of Paris's former abattoirs. This ultra-modern park includes two vast cultural complexes, one devoted to science and the other to music, themed gardens scattered with red metal follies and various children's activity areas. A long covered walk joins the main buildings.

## CITÉ DES SCIENCES ET DE L'INDUSTRIE

The abattoirs' former auction hall was transformed into a vast scientific complex surrounded by water in which the public is both spectator and actor. 'Explora' is a permanent exhibition centred on the earth and the universe, life, languages and communication, the use of natural resources and technological and industrial developments. The Cité des Enfants is a fascinating interactive world for children aged 3 to 12. There are also a planetarium, an aquarium, a 3-D cinema, a multimedia library, a research centre, a submarine, a simulation booth (Cinaxe), in which spectators are able to live through the action of a film, and La Géode, a huge sphere equipped with a hemispherical screen that shows films on scientific subjects.

### CITÉ DE LA MUSIQUE

The focal point of the Cité de la Musique is the vast square in front of the Grande Halle where concerts and exhibitions are held. On the left of the square is the National Conservatory of Music and Dance, while the triangular building on the right houses concerts halls and a museum (see Musée de la Musique ➤ 93).

✚ 124 D4 (off map) ✉ Cité des Sciences et de l'Industrie, parc de la Villette, 30 avenue Corentin Cariou, 75019; Cité de la Musique, 221 avenue Jean Jaurès, 75019 ☎ Cité des Sciences: 01 40 05 70 00; Cité de la Musique: information bookings 01 44 84 44 84 🕔 Cité des Sciences: Tue–Sat 10–6, Sun 10–7; closed 1 May, 25 Dec. Cité de la Musique: Tue–Sat 12–6, Sun 10–6 💷 Cité des Sciences: expensive; Cité de la Musique: free; museum: moderate
🍴 Restaurants nearby (€–€€) 🚇 Cité des Sciences: Porte de la Villette; Cité de la Musique: Porte de Pantin 🚌 Cité des Sciences: 75, 139, 150, 152, PC; Cité de la Musique: 75, 151, PC ❓ Cité des Sciences: exhibitions, lectures, shops; Cité de la Musique: themed tours, workshops, musical tours

# Exploring

GALERIES Lafayette

Galeries

The city of Paris has always played its role of capital of France to the full. It is where the French nation's future is decided, where revolutions began in the past and where major political, economic and social changes are traditionally launched. This is as true today as it ever was, in spite of many attempts at decentralization.

Parisian life reflects the city's leading role in many different ways: the numerous trade exhibitions and international conferences taking place every year testify to its economic and potitical dynamism and healthy competitive spirit. Paris is continually on the move in all fields of human activity: its architectural heritage is constantly expanding and it is proudly setting new trends in the arts, in gastronomy and in fashion. Paris is also a cosmopolitan metropolis where many ethnic groups find the necessary scope to express their differences.

# The Latin Quarter and the Islands

**Situated on the Left Bank between the Carrefour de l'Odéon and the Jardin des Plantes, the lively Latin Quarter was known in medieval times as the 'Montagne Ste-Geneviève' after the patron saint of Paris, and was later given the name of 'Quartier Latin' because Latin was spoken at the university until the late 18th century. To this day it remains the undisputed kingdom of Parisian students. The Sorbonne, the most famous French university**

**college, was founded in 1257; the present building dates from the late 19th century when well-known artists such as Puvis de Chavannes decorated the interior. The adjacent 17th-century church is a model of Jesuit style.**

The two river islands – Île de la Cité and Île St-Louis – have very different histories and characters. The Ile de la Cité is not only the historic centre of Paris, it is also a place of exceptional natural beauty and home to three major monuments – Notre-Dame, Sainte-Chapelle and the Conciergerie. The peaceful atmosphere of the Île St-Louis is apparent as soon as you walk along its shaded embankment, lined with elegant 17th-century mansions that stand as silent witnesses of a bygone era.

## CITÉ, ÎLE DE LA

The Celtic tribe the Parisii settled on the largest island in an area known as Lutetia, which under the Romans expanded onto the Left Bank of the Seine. Nevertheless, the island (the Cité), which the king of the Franks chose as his capital in AD 508, remained for 1,000 years the seat of royal, judicial and religious power. During the Middle Ages, the Île de la Cité was an important intellectual centre as its cathedral schools attracted students from all over Europe. Even after the kings of France left the royal palace for larger premises on the Right Bank, the Cité lost none of its symbolic importance and remains to this day the 'guardian' of 2,000 years of history.

The appearance of the Cité has changed considerably over the years; in the 19th century, the centre of the island was cleared and the vast square in front of Notre-Dame Cathedral created. At the

other end of the island, the Conciergerie and Sainte-Chapelle are the only remaining parts of the medieval royal palace, now incorporated in the huge Palais de Justice.

🚇 122 B4 ✉ Île de la Cité, 75001 and 75004 🍴 Restaurants and cafés (€–€€) on the island and on the Right and Left banks 🚇 Cité, Pont Neuf, St-Michel, Châtelet, Hôtel de Ville 🚌 21, 24, 27, 38, 47, 58, 70, 85, 96

### LA CONCIERGERIE

For most people, the name 'Conciergerie' suggests crowds of innocent prisoners waiting to be taken to the guillotine. Nowadays, its familiar round towers covered with conical slate roofs and the square clock tower, which housed the first public clock in Paris, are one of the most picturesque sights of the Île de la Cité. The Conciergerie is the last remaining authentic part of a 14th-century royal complex, administered by a *concierge* or governor. The twin towers marked the main entrance to the palace. In the late 14th century, the Conciergerie was turned into a prison but it only acquired a sinister connotation during the Revolution, when it held a number of famous prisoners, including Queen Marie-Antoinette, Madame du Barry and the poet André Chénier, as well as Danton and Robespierre. The visit includes the original guards' room, a magnificent great hall with Gothic vaulting and kitchens with monumental fireplaces. There is also a reconstruction of Marie-Antoinette's cell.

🚇 122 B4 ✉ 2 boulevard du Palais, 75001 ☎ 01 53 73 78 50 🕐 Daily 9.30–6. Closed 1 Jan, 1 May, 25 Dec 💷 Moderate 🚇 Cité, Châtelet 🚌 21, 24, 27, 38, 58, 85, 81, 85, 96, Balabus ❓ Guided tours, bookshop

## GOBELINS, MANUFACTURE NATIONALE DES

The former royal tapestry factory, founded by Colbert in 1664 to make beautiful tapestries for the royal household, is still going strong. Priceless works of art, based on paintings by artists such as Le Brun and Boucher and, more recently, Lurçat and Picasso, have been produced in the workshops over the last three centuries. Techniques have hardly changed since the 17th century and looms are either upright (*haute lice* method) or horizontal (*basse lice* method). The 17th-century buildings also house the Savonnerie carpet factory, founded in 1604, and the Beauvais tapestry factory, founded at the same time as the Gobelins.

✚ 122 F4 (off map) ✉ 42 avenue des Gobelins, 75013 ☎ 01 44 54 19 33; 01 44 08 52 00 🕐 Tue, Wed, Thu guided tours only at 2 and 2.45. Closed public hols 👖 Moderate 🚇 Les Gobelins 🚌 27, 47, 83, 91

## INSTITUT DU MONDE ARABE

The Institute of Arab and Islamic Civilization is a remarkable piece of modern architecture designed by the French architect Jean Nouvel. Its glass-and-aluminium façade, reminiscent of a *musharabia* (carved wooden screen), discretely refers to Arab tradition. The seventh floor houses a museum of Islamic art and civilization from the 8th century to the present day. The ninth floor offers a panoramic view of the Île de la Cité and Île St-Louis near by.

✚ 123 D5 ✉ 1 rue des Fossés St-Bernard, 75005 ☎ 01 40 51 38 38 🕐 Tue–Sun 10–6. Closed 1 May 👖 Inexpensive 🍴 Restaurant (€–€€) 🚇 Jussieu 🚌 24, 63, 67, 86, 87, 89 ❓ Guided tours, shops

ENTRÉE
EXPOSITION

ENTRÉE
PRINCIPALE

## MOYEN-AGE, MUSÉE NATIONAL DU

The museum, also known as the Musée de Cluny, is housed in the 15th-century Hôtel de Cluny, one of the last examples of medieval domestic architecture in Paris, and stands at the heart of the Quartier Latin. Inside the main courtyard, the elegant stair tower and corner turrets are noteworthy. The most famous of the museum's exhibits of medieval arts and crafts is a set of 15th-century tapestries known as 'La Dame à la Licorne'. There is also a fine collection of sculptures, including the heads of the kings of Judaea that decorated the façade of Notre-Dame Cathedral and were knocked down during the Revolution. The museum is built on the site of 3rd century AD Gallo-Roman baths, and visitors can see the remains of the *frigidarium*. The ruins are surrounded by a public garden.

**www.**musee-moyenage.fr

✚ 122 C3 ✉ 6 place Paul Painlevé, 75005 ☎ 01 53 73 78 00; 01 53 73 78 16 ⏰ Wed–Mon 9.15–5.45. Closed 1 Jan, 1 May, 25 Dec 💷 Inexpensive 🍴 Boulevard St-Michel nearby (€–€€) Ⓜ Cluny-La Sorbonne 🚌 21, 27, 38, 63, 85, 86, 87 ❓ Guided tours, shops, concerts

## NOTRE-DAME

See pages 32–33.

## PANTHÉON

Commissioned by Louis XV, the building was meant to replace
St Genevieve's Church in the Quartier Latin; designed by Soufflot,
who gave it the shape of a Greek cross surmounted by a high
dome, it is now one of Paris's landmarks. Completed on the eve
of the Revolution, it became a Pantheon for France's illustrious
dead, among them Voltaire, Rousseau, Hugo, Zola, and more
recently Jean Moulin (head of the French Resistance during World
War II) and André Malraux (writer and highly successful Minister
of Culture).

🕂 122 D4 ✉ Place du Panthéon, 75005 ☎ 01 44 32 18 00 🕐 Apr–Sep daily
10–6.30; Oct–Mar daily 10–6. Closed 1 Jan, 1 May, 25 Dec ✋ Moderate
🚇 Cardinal-Lemoine 🚌 84, 89 ❓ Shops

LA CONVENTION NATIONALE

## PLANTES, JARDIN DES

Today the botanical gardens, which owe their name to the 'royal garden of medicinal plants' created in the 17th century, form the experimental gardens of the Musée National d'Histoire Naturelle (Natural History Museum). This is an ideal place for a leisurely stroll; children love the *ménagerie* (zoo). There are also hothouses, an alpine garden and several exhibition halls, the most fascinating being the Grande Galerie de l'Evolution, illustrating the evolution of life on earth and Man's influence on it. Here, the display of endangered and extinct species is particularly interesting. Also featured are the scientists closely associated with evolution and the latest discoveries in the field of genetics.

✚ 123 E6 ✉ 57 rue Cuvier, 75005 ☎ 01 40 79 30 00 🕐 Gardens: daily 7.30–sunset. Museum: Wed–Mon 10–5. Zoo: daily 9–6 ✋ Gardens: free; museum and zoo: moderate 🍴 Cafeteria (€) 🚇 Jussieu ❓ Lectures, exhibitions, workshops for children, shop

## LES QUAIS

See pages 37–37.

## ST-ETIENNE-DU-MONT

The Church of St-Etienne-du-Mont, dating from the late 15th century, combines Flamboyant Gothic and Renaissance styles. Don't miss the delicately fretted rood-screen inside.

✚ 122 D4 ✉ Place Ste-Geneviève, 75005 🕐 Jul–Aug Tue–Sun 10–12, 4–7.15; Sep–Jun Mon–Sat 8.30–12, 2–7.15 ✋ Free 🚇 Cardinal Lemoine 🚌 84, 89

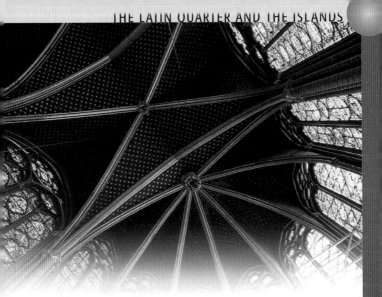

## SAINTE-CHAPELLE

The full splendour of this magnificent Gothic chapel, surely Paris's most beautiful church, can only be appreciated from inside, as Sainte-Chapelle is unfortunately closely surrounded by the Palais de Justice buildings. Commissioned by Louis IX, a king so devout that he came to be known as Saint Louis, to house the Crown of Thorns and a fragment of the true Cross, it was built in less than three years by Pierre de Montreuil (who also worked on Notre-Dame) and was consecrated in 1248.

The building consists of two chapels, the lower one intended as a parish church for the palace staff and the upper one reserved for the royal family. The latter is a striking example of technical prowess: walls have been replaced by 15m-high (49ft) stained-glass panels linked by slender pillars which also support the vaulting. The stained-glass windows, which cover an area of more than 600sq m (6,460sq ft), are mainly original and illustrate scenes from the Old and New Testaments.

➕ 122 B3 ✉ 4 boulevard du Palais, 75001 ☎ 01 53 40 60 80 🕐 Oct–Mar daily 10–5; Apr–Sep daily 9.30–6.30. Closed 1 Jan, 1 May, 1 Nov
✋ Moderate 🚇 Cité 🚌 96 ❓ Shop

### ST-LOUIS, ÎLE

The island was formed at the beginning of
the 17th century, when two small islands
were united and joined to the mainland by
a couple of bridges linked by the rue des
Deux Ponts, which still exists; at the
same time, private residences were built
along the embankment and the straight
narrow streets. The whole project was
completed in a remarkably short time
between 1627 and 1664. Since then, time
seems to have stood still on the Île Saint-
Louis, which to this day retains its
provincial character.

A few architectural gems can be seen
along quai de Bourbon and quai d'Anjou,
which offer fine views of the Right Bank. From the western tip of
the island you can see Notre-Dame and the Île de la Cité. Concerts
are regularly given in the Classical Church of St-Louis-en-l'Île, richly
decorated inside.

➕ 123 C6 ✉ 75004 🍴 Rue St-Louis-en-l'Île (€€) 🚇 Pont Marie 🚌 67, 86,
87

### ST-SÉVERIN

St-Séverin is one of the most beautiful churches in the capital,
with its delightful blend of Flamboyant Gothic architecture and
contemporary stained glass. It dates originally from the 13th
century and is dedicated to the 6th-century hermit St Séverin, who
was closely associated with St Martin, patron saint of travellers.
The surrounding cobbled streets, full of cafés, shops and cheap
eateries, are popular with students and visitors alike.
**www.**saint-severin.com

➕ 122 C4 ✉ 1 rue des Prêtres-St-Séverin, 75005 ☎ 01 42 34 93 50
🕐 Mon–Sat 11–7.30, Sun 9–8.30 🚇 Saint-Michel

# Eiffel Tower to St-Germain-des-Prés

**The Rive Gauche (Left Bank), with its narrow streets lined with shops and restaurants, and its breathtaking monuments, exudes Parisian charm. It's one of the most sought-after residential districts in Paris and eternally magnetic to both visitors and residents.**

The Left Bank in this chapter comprises the area from the Tour Eiffel in the west to the Jardin du Luxembourg in the east, and south to include Montparnasse, popular with artists and writers in the early 20th century. Some of the city's best-known attractions are found here – the Musée d'Orsay, housed in a magnificent Industrial Age train terminus, the atmospheric Quartier St-Germain-des-Prés, with its literary associations, the imposing architectural ensemble of Les Invalides, and that marvel of 19th-century engineering, the Eiffel Tower.

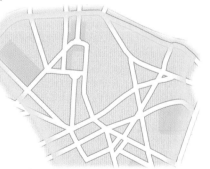

## ASSEMBLÉE NATIONALE PALAIS-BOURBON

The façade of this neoclassical building, housing the lower house of the French parliament, echoes that of the Madeleine across the place de la Concorde. Completed by Louis XV's famous architect Gabriel, the Palais-Bourbon still bears the name of the French royal family to whom it once belonged. Guided tours (identity document required) include the chamber, where members of parliament sit on benches arranged in semicircular tiers, several reception rooms and the library, richly decorated by Delacroix.

➕ 120 A4 ✉ 33 quai d'Orsay, 75007 ☎ 01 40 63 60 08 🕐 Guided tours only Sat 10am, 2pm, 3pm. Closed public hols and when Parliament is sitting 💷 Free 🚇 Assemblée Nationale 🚌 63, 83, 84, 94 ❓ Shops

## EUGÈNE DELACROIX, MUSÉE NATIONAL

The old-world charm of the tiny rue de Furstenberg, hidden behind the Church of St-Germain-des-Prés, is the perfect setting for a museum devoted to one of the major French Romantic painters. Delacroix lived and worked here until the end of his life and, besides a few paintings, the place is full of mementoes of the artist, letters, sketches...and his palette. There is also a bookshop. It is well worth taking time to explore the picturesque neighbourhood and the open market in rue de Buci.
www.musee-delacroix.fr

➕ 121 B7 ✉ 6 rue de Furstenberg, 75006 ☎ 01 44 41 86 50 🕐 Wed–Mon 9.30–5. Closed public hols 💷 Inexpensive 🚇 St-Germain-des-Prés 🚌 39, 48, 63, 95

## FAUBOURG ST-GERMAIN

This 'suburb' is today one of the most elegant districts of central Paris. Its name came from the nearby Abbaye de St-Germain-des-Prés to which it belonged in medieval times. University students loved to stroll through the meadows stretching down to the river west of the abbey and the area remained in its natural state until the 18th century, when it became fashionable for the aristocracy and the wealthy middle class to have mansions built there by the famous architects of the time.

The rue de Varenne is lined with the famous Hôtel Matignon, now the prime minister's residence, and the Hôtel Biron, better known as the Musée Rodin (➤ 63). The parallel rue de Grenelle is interesting for its wealth of authentic architecture, including the Hôtel de Villars, now the town hall of the 7th *arrondissement*. Further along, on the opposite side, is an interesting museum (No 59) devoted to the sculptor Maillol (➤ 60).

✚ 121 B7 ✉ 75007 🕐 For the museums' opening times, see the relevant entries 🍽 Cafés and restaurants nearby in boulevard St-Germain (€–€€) 🚇 Varenne, Rue du Bac 🚌 69, 83, 84, 94

## INSTITUT DE FRANCE

The imposing Classical building facing the Louvre across the river was commissioned by Cardinal Mazarin as a school for provincial children, and designed by Le Vau; it is topped by a magnificent dome and houses the Institut de France, created in 1795 to unite under one roof five prestigious academies, including the Académie Française, founded in 1635 by Richelieu. It also houses the Bibliothèque Mazarine, Mazarin's own collection of rare editions.

✚ 121 B8 ✉ 23 quai de Conti, 75006 ☎ 01 44 41 44 35 🕐 Sat, Sun guided tours by appointment only 💷 Inexpensive 🚇 Pont Neuf, Louvre, Odéon 🚌 24, 27, 39, 48, 58, 70, 95

## LES INVALIDES

See pages 28–29.

## LUXEMBOURG, JARDIN DU

Just a stone's throw from the Sorbonne, this
attractive French-style garden is traditionally the
haunt of students and lovers, who particularly
favour the area surrounding the Fontaine
de Médicis, named after Marie de
Médicis, who commissioned the Palais
du Luxembourg (now the Senate) and
the gardens.

✚ 121 D7 ✉ Boulevard St-Michel, 75006
☎ 01 42 34 23 62 🕙 Apr–Oct daily
7am–7.30pm; Mar and Nov daily 8–dusk
🚇 Luxembourg

## MAILLOL, MUSÉE

This atttractive museum, in the rue de Grenelle next to a beautiful
18th-century fountain, is interesting on two accounts: it displays a
great many works by the French painter and sculptor Aristide
Maillol (1861–1944), as well as a private collection of works by
Ingres, Cézanne, Dufy, Matisse, Bonnard, Degas, Picasso,
Gauguin, Rodin, Kandinsky and Poliakoff among others. Maillol's
obsessive theme was the nude, upon which he conferred an
allegorical meaning; he produced smooth rounded figures, some
of which can be seen in the Jardin des Tuileries.

✚ 121 B6 ✉ 61 rue de Grenelle, 75007 ☎ 01 42 22 59 58 🕙 Wed–Mon
11–6. Closed public hols ✋ Moderate 🍴 Cafeteria (€) 🚇 Rue du Bac
🚌 63, 68, 69, 83, 84 ❓ Shop

## MONTPARNASSE

Fashions change quickly in artistic circles and, soon after the turn
of the 20th century, young artists and writers left Montmartre to
settle on the Left Bank, in an area which had been known as
Montparnasse since medieval times. Modigliani, Chagall, Léger
and many others found studios in La Ruche, the counterpart of the

Bateau-Lavoir in Montmartre (➤ 90). They were later joined by Russian political refugees, musicians and, between the wars, American writers of the 'lost generation', among them Hemingway. They met in cafés along boulevard Montparnasse, which have since become household names: La Closerie des Lilas, La Rotonde, Le Select, La Coupole and Le Dôme.

Since the 1960s the district has been modernized and a business complex built south of the boulevard. The 200m-high (656ft) **Tour Montparnasse** stands in front of one of the busiest stations in Paris. The tower's 56th and 59th floors are open to the public and offer a restaurant and panoramic views.

➕ 121 F5 ✉ 75014 Ⓜ Montparnasse-Bienvenüe, Vavin

**Tour Montparnasse**
➕ 121 E5 ✉ Rue de l'Arrivée, 75015 ☎ 01 45 38 52 56 ⓒ Daily 9.30am–10.30pm (11.30pm in summer) 👑 Moderate 🍴 Le Ciel de Paris (€€)

### ORSAY, MUSÉE D'
See pages 34–35.

## RODIN, MUSÉE

Rodin spent the last few years of his life in the Hôtel Biron as a guest of the French nation; when he died the collection of his works reverted to the State and the mansion was turned into a museum. His forceful and highly original style brought him many disappointments and failures: his *Man with a Broken Nose* (now in the museum) was refused at the 1864 Salon and Rodin had to wait for another 15 years before his talent was fully acknowledged through his *St John the Baptist*. His major works are inside the museum *(The Kiss, Man Walking)* and in the gardens *(The Thinker, The Burghers of Calais, The Gates of Hell)*.

www.musee-rodin.fr

✚ 120 B4 ✉ 77 rue de Varenne, 75007 ☎ 01 44 18 61 10 🕐 Tue–Sun 9.30–4.45 (5.45 in summer, park 6.45). Closed 1 Jan, 25 Dec 💷 Inexpensive 🍴 Cafeteria (€) 🚇 Varenne, Invalides, Saint-François-Xavier 🚌 69, 82, 87, 92 ❓ Guided tours, shops

## ST-GERMAIN-DES-PRÉS

The Benedictine Abbey of St-Germain-des-Prés, founded in the 6th century, was throughout the Middle Ages so powerful a religious and cultural centre that it became a town within the town. It was completely destroyed during the Revolution; only the church was spared. In spite of many alterations, the church is a fine example of Romanesque style: the tower dates from the 11th century as does the nave; note that the carved capitals on the pillars are copies of the originals kept in the Musée National du Moyen-Âge (➤ 50). The chancel and ambulatory date from the 12th century.

It is worth exploring the old streets on the north and east sides of the church and strolling along boulevard St-Germain. The area between boulevard St-Germain and the river and between rue du Bac and rue de Seine is full of antique shops and art galleries.

✚ 121 C7 ✉ Place St-Germain-des-Prés, 75006 ☎ 01 55 42 81 33 🕐 Daily 8–7 💷 Free 🍴 Cafés/restaurants near by (€–€€) 🚇 St-Germain-des-Prés

### ST-SULPICE

The original church, founded by the Abbey of St-Germain-des-Prés, was rebuilt and extended in the 17th century but was not completed until the mid-18th century. The Italian-style façade, designed by Servandoni, is surmounted by two slightly different towers crowned by balustrades and is in marked contrast to the rest of the building. Among the wealth of interior decoration are several statues by Bouchardon and outstanding murals by Delacroix (first chapel on the right) as well as a splendid organ by Cavaillé-Coll, traditionally played by the best organists in France. Servandoni had also submitted plans for the square in front of the church, but they were abandoned and a monumental fountain designed by Visconti was eventually placed in its centre in 1844.

➕ 121 C7 ✉ Place St-Sulpice, 75006 ☎ 01 46 33 21 78 🕐 Daily 7.30–7.30
✋ Free 🚇 St-Sulpice

### LA TOUR EIFFEL

See pages 38–39.

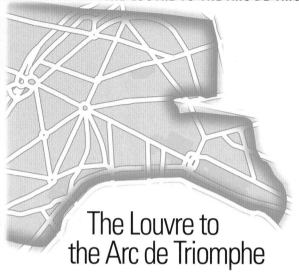

# The Louvre to the Arc de Triomphe

**The area of western Paris, from the Louvre to the Arc de Triomphe is noted more for its grandeur than its charm. It's full of elegant squares, formal gardens, fashionable shops and luxury hotels.**

Without a doubt, the greatest attraction is the Musée du Louvre. Northwest lie the Jardin des Tuileries, place de la Concorde and the Champs-Élysées, which leads to the Arc de Triomphe and on to La Défense. South of the Arc de Triomphe brings you to the Palais de Chaillot, while north of the Louvre are two of Paris's best shopping streets – rue de Rivoli and rue St-Honoré.

## ALEXANDRE III, PONT

This is Paris's most ornate bridge, named after the Tsar of Russia to celebrate the Franco-Russian alliance. Its sole arch spanning the Seine is in line with the Invalides on the Left Bank while, on the Right Bank, the avenue Winston Churchill leads straight to the Champs-Elysées. The bridge is decorated with exuberant allegorical sculptures surmounted by gilt horses.

✠ 117 F6 ✉ Cours La Reine/Quai d'Orsay 🚇 Invalides 🚌 63, 83

## ARC DE TRIOMPHE

Commissioned by Napoleon, the 50m-high (164ft) Arc de Triomphe was completed by France's last reigning monarch and finally dedicated to the memory of an unknown soldier of the Republic who died during World War I. It stands in line with the Arc de Triomphe du Carrousel near the Louvre and the Grande Arche de la Défense. From the top there is a 360-degree panorama, with, in the foreground, its 12 avenues reaching out like tentacles towards the city beyond.

🕂 116 C3 ⊠ Place Charles de Gaulle, 75008 ☎ 01 43 80 31 31 🕙 Oct–Mar daily 10am–10.30pm; Apr–Sep daily 10am–11pm. Closed 1 Jan, 1 May, 25 Dec 🖐 Moderate 🍴 Choice of restaurants near by (€–€€€) 🚇 Charles de Gaulle-Etoile 🚌 22, 30, 31, 52, 78, 92 ❓ Video, shops

## ART MODERNE DE LA VILLE DE PARIS, MUSÉE D'

The Palais de Tokyo, housing the modern art collections, was built for the 1937 World Exhibition; significantly, one of the main exhibits is a huge work called *La Fée Electricité*, painted by Raoul Dufy for the 'Light Pavilion' at the Exhibition. Most of the major artisitic trends of the 20th century are represented.

🕂 116 F3 ⊠ 11 avenue du Président Wilson, 75116 ☎ 01 53 67 40 00 🕙 Tue–Fri 10–5.30, Sat–Sun 10–7. Closed public hols 🖐 Inexpensive 🍴 Cafe (€) 🚇 Iéna, Alma-Marceau 🚌 32, 42, 63, 72, 80, 92 ❓ Guided tours (reservations necessary)

## ARTS ASIATIQUES-GUIMET, MUSÉE NATIONAL DES/PANTHÉON BOUDDHIQUE

This museum's collections, spanning 5,000 years, illustrate all the major civilizations of the Asian continent, with special emphasis on calligraphy, painting, gold plate and textiles. In addition, carefully restored monumental works from Cambodia and Afghanistan are on display for the first time.

**www.**museeguimet.fr

✚ 116 E3 ✉ Museum: 6 place d'Iéna; Panthéon Bouddhique: 19 avenue d'Iéna, 75016 ☎ 01 56 52 53 00 🕐 Wed–Mon 10–6 ✋ Moderate
🚇 Boissiére, Iéna 🚌 22, 30, 32, 63, 82

## ARTS DÉCORATIFS, MUSÉE DES

The Museum of Decorative Arts is housed in the Marsan wing of the Louvre. The Medieval and Renaissance collections include remarkable altarpieces, religious paintings, 16th-century stained-glass objects of daily life, and fine tapestries.

✚ 118 F3 ✉ 107 rue de Rivoli, 75001 ☎ 01 44 55 57 50 🕐 Tue–Fri 11–6, Sat–Sun 10–6 ✋ Inexpensive 🍴 The main Louvre nearby 🚇 Palais-Royal
🚌 21, 27, 39, 48, 68, 72, 81, 95

## BACCARAT, MUSÉE

The museum's collections of Baccarat crystal illustrate the evolution of styles and manufacturing techniques since 1764: vases, chandeliers, perfume bottles and other objects. The most fascinating exhibits are probably the unique pieces specially created by Baccarat for various World Exhibitions since 1855.

✚ 116 E3 ✉ 11 place des Etats-Unis, 75016 ☎ 01 40 22 11 00 🕐 Mon, Wed–Sat 10–6 ✋ Inexpensive 🚇 Iéna, Boissière 🚌 32, 38 48

## BALZAC, MAISON DE

Honoré de Balzac lived here from 1840 to 1847. It contains mementoes of his life and work, such as manuscripts, letters, original drawings and prints and a plaster cast that Rodin used as a study for the monumental statue now standing in Montparnasse.

✚ 116 F1 (off map) ✉ 47 rue Raynouard, 75016 ☎ 01 55 74 41 80
🕐 Tue–Sun 10–6. Closed public hols ✋ Free 🚇 Passy, La Muette 🚌 32, 50, 70, 72

## CERNUSCHI, MUSÉE

The building houses banker and art collector Henri Cernuschi's superb collection of ancient Chinese art on the ground floor (terracottas, bronzes, jades and ceramics) and contemporary traditional Chinese paintings on the first floor.

✚ 117 B6 ✉ 7 avenue Velasquez, 75008 ☎ 01 45 63 50 75 ⏱ Tue–Sun 10–5.40 💰 Inexpensive Ⓜ Villiers 🚌 30, 94

## CHAILLOT, PALAIS DE

Designed for the 1937 World Exhibition, the building consists of two separate pavilions with curved wings, on either side of a vast terrace decorated with monumental statues. Just below, the tiered Jardins du Trocadéro extend to the edge of the river. The spotlit ornamental fountain is particularly impressive at night.

The Musée de l'Homme, devoted to Man as a species, contains items from Africa, Asia and South America, including around 500 musical instruments from around the world.

The Musée de la Marine is devoted to French maritime history from the 18th century onwards. The extensive collections show the development of navigational skills and include models of 18th-century sailing ships; they also retrace the history of maritime transport and great expeditions across the world.

The Cité de l'Architecture et du Patrimoine promotes awareness of modern architecture, exploring influential architectural trends and examining the work of key architects. Visitors can also see casts from the Musée des Monuments Français.

**www.mnhn.fr**

✚ 116 F2 ✉ Place du Trocadéro, 75016 ☎ Musée de l'Homme: 01 44 05 72 72; Musée de la Marine: 01 53 65 69 69; Cité de l'Architecture et du Patrimoine: 01 58 51 52 00 ⏱ Musée de l'Homme: Wed–Mon 9.45–5.15, Sat–Sun 10–6.30; closed public hols. Musée de la Marine: Wed–Mon 10–6; closed 1 Jan, 1 May, 25 Dec; Cité de l'Architecture et du Patrimoine: Mon, Wed, Fri noon–8, Thu noon–10, Sat–Sun 11–7 💰 Moderate Ⓜ Trocadéro 🚌 22, 30, 32, 63, 72, 82

### CHAMPS-ELYSÉES, LES

See pages 24–25.

### CONCORDE, PLACE DE LA

This is undoubtedly the most impressive square in Paris: its stately elegance, its size and its magnificent views are simply breathtaking. Built in the mid-18th century, it was designed by Gabriel who erected two Classical pavilions on either side of the rue Royale; its octagonal shape is emphasized by eight allegorical statues representing major French cities.

The pink granite obelisk from Luxor, offered to the French nation by the viceroy of Egypt in 1836, is at the centre of the square, flanked by two graceful fountains. Two magnificent vistas open up: one towards the Champs-Elysées and Le Louvre beyond the beautiful gates of the Jardin des Tuileries; the other towards the Madeleine at the end of the rue Royale and the Assemblée Nationale across the pont de la Concorde.

➕ 117 E7 ✉ 75008 🚇 Concorde 🚌 42, 73, 84, 94

## FAUBOURG ST-HONORÉ

This 'suburb' is centred on the very long street of the same name, running parallel to the Champs-Elysées and famous for its haute couture establishments and luxury boutiques as well as for the Palais de l'Elysée, the official residence of the French president.

Leading fashion houses have been established in the area for over a hundred years: Louis Féraud, Christian Lacroix and Lanvin are still in the rue du Faubourg St-Honoré, but the majority are now in the avenue Montaigne across the Champs-Elysées. Opposite the British Embassy, No 54 opens into a couple of courtyards surrounded by boutiques selling beautiful furniture, objets d'art and paintings. Many modern art galleries line the perpendicular avenue Matignon, while the avenue Gabriel, which runs along the Champs-Elysées gardens past the American Embassy, makes a peaceful stroll through this select area.

✚ 117 D6 ✉ 75008 🚇 St-Philippe-du-Roule, Madeleine
🚌 52 ❓ A stamp market takes place near the Rond-Point des Champs-Elysées on Thu, Sat and Sun 9–7

## GALLIÉRA, MUSÉE

This museum of fashion is housed in a neo-Renaissance mansion dating from the late 19th century, the Palais Galliéra. Its rich collections of urban fashion, are shown in temporary exhibitions from the 18th century to the present and are continually being extended with donations from prestigious fashion houses (Dior, Yves St-Laurent) and well-known personalities. In addition to the costumes (several thousand in all), there are etchings and photographs connected with fashion.

✚ 116 E3 ✉ Palais Galliéra, 10 avenue Pierre Ier de Serbie, 75016 ☎ 01 56 52 86 20 🕐 Tue–Sun 10–6 💰 Moderate 🚇 Iéna 🚌 32, 42, 63, 72, 80, 82, 92 ❓ Children's workshops

## GRAND PALAIS

Built at the same time as the Pont Alexandre III for the 1900 World Exhibition, this enormous steel-and-glass structure, concealed behind stone walls, is typical of the *belle époque* style: Ionic columns line the imposing façade and colossal bronze statues decorate the four corners. Major international art exhibitions – Tutankhamun, Renoir, Gauguin and Picasso, to name but a few – are traditionally held in the Galeries Nationales, on the Champs-Elysées side of the building.

The west part of the Grand Palais houses the Palais de la Découverte, inaugurated in 1937 to bring science within the grasp of the general public and keep them informed of the latest scientific developments. There are interactive experiments, documentary films and a planetarium.

➕ 117 E6 ✉ Galeries Nationales: avenue du Général Eisenhower, 75008; Palais de la Découverte, avenue Franklin-D-Roosevelt, 75008 ☎ Galeries Nationales: 01 44 13 17 30; Palais Découverte: 01 56 43 20 21 🕐 Galeries Nationales: variable; Palais Découverte: Tue–Sat 9.30–6, Sun 10–7 ✋ Galeries Nationales: variable; Palais Découverte: moderate 🍴 Café-bar (€) Ⓜ Champs-Elysées-Clemenceau 🚌 28, 32, 42, 72, 73, 80, 83, 93

## LA GRANDE ARCHE DE LA DÉFENSE

See pages 26–27.

### JACQUEMART-ANDRÉ, MUSÉE

This elegant 19th-century mansion houses
the remarkable collections of European art
bequeathed by the wealthy widow of a banker
to the Institut de France. French 18th-century
art includes paintings by Boucher, Chardin,
Greuze and Watteau, as well as sculptures
by Houdon and Pigalle, furniture, Beauvais
tapestries and objets d'art. There are also
17th-century Dutch and Flemish masterpieces
and Italian Renaissance art including works by
Mantegna, Donatello, Botticelli and Uccello.

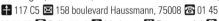

✚ 117 C5 ✉ 158 boulevard Haussmann, 75008 ☎ 01 45
62 11 59 ⊙ Daily 10–6 🖐 Moderate 🍴 Tea room (€) Ⓜ Miromesnil,
St-Philippe-du-Roule 🚌 22, 28, 43, 52, 54, 80, 83, 84, 93

### JEU DE PAUME

One of two pavilions built in the late 19th century at the entrance
of the Jardin des Tuileries, the Jeu de Paume was intended for the
practice of a game similar to tennis. It later housed the national
collection of Impressionist paintings until it was transferred to the
Musée d'Orsay. Now it is now exclusively devoted to the art of
photography, holding thematic and monographic exhibitions from
the 19th century to the 21st century.

✚ 117 E8 ✉ 1 place de la Concorde, 75001 ☎ 01 47 03 12 52 ⊙ Wed–Fri
12–7, Sat–Sun 10–7, Tue 12–9.30 🖐 Moderate 🍴 Café (€) Ⓜ Concorde
🚌 24, 42, 52, 72, 73, 84, 94 ❓ Shop

### LE LOUVRE

See pages 30–31.

### MADELEINE, ÉGLISE DE LA

Work started on this imposing neoclassical building in 1764, and
the church was eventually consecrated in 1845. An impressive

Graeco-Roman temple completely surrounded by tall Corinthian columns, the church is one of the city's landmarks. Steps lead up to the entrance, which is surmounted by a monumental pediment. The interior is decorated with sculptures by Rude and Pradier; the magnificent organ was made by Cavaillé-Coll in 1846.

➕ 117 D8 ✉ Place de la Madeleine, 75008 ☎ 01 44 51 69 00 🕒 Mon–Sat 7–7, Sun 8–1.30, 3.30–7; public hols variable ✋ Free 🚇 Madeleine 🚌 24, 42, 52, 84, 94 ❓ Shops

## MARMOTTAN-MONET, MUSÉE

The museum was named after Paul Marmottan, who bequeathed his house and his private collections of Renaissance and 18th- and 19th-century art to the Institut de France. These were later enriched by several bequests, including 100 paintings by Monet donated by his son: detailed studies of Monet's garden in Giverny,

particularly a group of *nymphéas* (water lilies) paintings, provide insights into the artist's approach, and there are paintings of Rouen Cathedral (executed in different light conditions according to the time of day) and of the River Thames in London. Most important of all, perhaps, is a relatively early work, called *Impression, Soleil levant* (1872), which created a sensation at the time and gave its name to the Impressionist movement. There are also interesting works by Monet's contemporaries, Renoir, Pissarro, Sisley, Morisot and Gauguin.

➕ 116 F1 (off map) ✉ 2 rue Louis Boilly, 75016 ☎ 01 42 24 07 02 🕒 Tue–Sun 10–6. Closed 1 Jan, 1 May, 25 Dec ✋ Moderate 🍴 Cafés and restaurants (€–€€) in nearby place de la Muette 🚇 La Muette 🚌 22, 32, 52, 63 ❓ Shops

### NISSIM DE CAMONDO, MUSÉE

This museum offers a delightful journey back into the 18th century. The interior is arranged as an authentic 18th-century private home, including wall panelling, Aubusson and Savonnerie tapestries, paintings by Vigée-Lebrun and Hubert Robert, sculptures by Houdon and Sèvres and Chantilly porcelain.

🔋 117 B6 🖂 63 rue de Monceau, 75008 ☎ 01 53 89 06 50 🕐 Wed–Sun 10–5. Closed 1 Jan, 14 Jul, 25 Dec 🖐 Inexpensive 🚇 Villiers 🚌 84, 94 ❓ Guided tours

### OPÉRA GARNIER

The Palais Garnier (named after its architect) was built in 1875 in neoclassical style, but the decoration is unmistakably late 19th century and includes a group of statues called *La Danse* by Carpeaux, a copy of the original now in the Musée d'Orsay. Inside, the grand staircase and the foyer are magnificent. In the main hall, restored to its original splendour, visitors can now fully appreciate the ceiling decorated by Chagall.

The museum contains paintings, watercolours and pastels illustrating the history of opera and ballet from the 18th century to the present day, mainly through portraits of famous singers, dancers and composers.

🔋 118 D3 🖂 Place de l'Opéra, 75009 ☎ 01 41 10 08 10 🕐 Daily 10–4.30. Closed 1 Jan, 1 May and matinee performances 🖐 Moderate 🚇 Opéra 🚌 20, 21, 22, 27, 29, 42, 52, 53, 56, 81, 95 ❓ Guided tours at 12.30, shops

### ORANGERIE, MUSÉE NATIONAL DE L'

The Orangerie houses the Walter-Guillaume Collection, consisting mainly of Impressionist and 20th-century paintings, and a set of monumental paintings by Monet, representing the famous *nymphéas* (water lilies) in the artist's garden at Giverny.

➕ 117 F7 ✉ Place de la Concorde, Jardin des Tuileries, 75001 ☎ 01 42 97 48 16 🕓 Closed for restructuring Ⓜ Concorde 🚌 24, 42, 52, 72, 73, 84, 94 ❓ Guided tours, shops

### PALAIS-ROYAL

The palace built by Richelieu and bequeathed to the king on the cardinal's death now houses the Ministry of Culture and two important constitutional bodies, but the gardens are accessible through archways situated all round. Enclosed by arcading on three sides and an elegant double colonnade along the fourth,

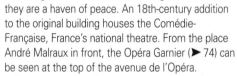

they are a haven of peace. An 18th-century addition to the original building houses the Comédie-Française, France's national theatre. From the place André Malraux in front, the Opéra Garnier (▶ 74) can be seen at the top of the avenue de l'Opéra.

To the east of the Palais-Royal, off the rue Croix des Petits Champs, the Galerie Véro-Dodat is one of several elegant arcades in the area.

➕ 118 F4 ✉ Place du Palais-Royal, 75001 🕓 Jardin: daily 8am–11pm (midnight in summer) ♿ Jardin: free access 🍴 In the gardens (€€) Ⓜ Palais-Royal

### PARFUM, MUSÉE DU

The museum traces the history of perfume from ancient Egypt to the present day. It is housed within the Fragonard perfumery, on two sites, both near the opera house.

**www.**fragonard.com

➕ 118 D3 ✉ 9 rue Scribe, 75009; 39 boulevard des Capucines, 75002 ♿ Free

## TUILERIES, JARDIN DES

This formal French-style garden was laid out by Le Nôtre in the 17th century. It deteriorated over the years through extensive use and the increasing effects of pollution, but has been renovated. The stately central alleyway stretches in a straight line from the flower beds near the Arc de Triomphe du Carrousel to the place de la Concorde, where an octagonal ornamental pool is surrounded by various statues and flanked by terraces. On either side of the alleyway are groups of allegorical statues. There is a lovely view of the river and the gardens with the Louvre in the background from the Terrasse du Bord de l'Eau running along the riverbank.

✚ 117 F8 ✉ Rue de Rivoli, 75001 🕐 Apr–Sep daily 7.30am–8pm; Oct–Mar daily 7.30am–7pm 🖐 Free 🍴 Cafeterias (€) 🚇 Tuileries (access from rue de Rivoli); Palais-Royal (access from the Louvre) 🚌 24, 68, 72, 73, 84, 94

## VENDÔME, PLACE

This square illustrates Louis XIV's style at its best, Classical and elegant without being too emphatic. It was designed by Jules Hardouin-Mansart at the end of the 17th century and an equestrian statue of the King was placed in its centre. However, the statue was destroyed during the Revolution and in 1810 Napoleon had a tall bronze-clad column erected in its place, somewhat spoiling the architectural harmony. Today Paris's top jewellers are based here.

✚ 118 E3 ✉ 75001 🚇 Opéra 🚌 72

# Le Marais and Bastille

**Le Marais was once an area of marshland on the Right Bank of the Seine. In the 13th century, the area was drained and cultivated by monks and the Knights Templar. However, it was the construction of the place des Vosges at the beginning of the 17th century and the subsequent rapid urbanization of the district that produced a wealth of beautiful domestic architecture and gave Le Marais its unique character. When fashions changed in the late 18th century, the district gradually became derelict and had to wait until the 1970s to be rediscovered and renovated.**

To the west is the Beaubourg district, renowned for its ultra-modern Les Halles shopping centre, and the Centre Georges Pompidou, with its world-famous art collections. To the east lies the Bastille district, forever associated with the French Revolution when the dreaded fortress was stormed by the people of Paris on 14 July, 1789, and later razed to the ground. Today the area is a lively nightspot with a great selection of bars and restaurants. Further east, on the edge of the city, is Cimetière du Père-Lachaise, Paris's most famous cemetery.

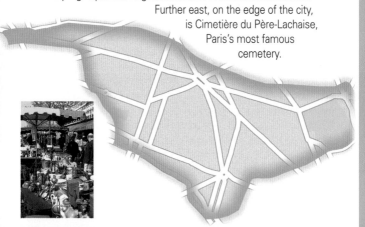

## ARTS ET MÉTIERS-TECHNIQUES, MUSÉE DES

This quirky museum is devoted to the artistic aspect of scientific and technical achievements.

✚ 119 E7 ✉ 60 rue Réaumur, 75003 ☎ 01 53 01 82 00 🕐 Tue–Sun 10–6 (Thu to 9.30pm) ✋ Moderate 🚇 Arts et Métiers

## BASTILLE

The outline of the Bastille can be seen on the paving stones covering the entire place de la Bastille. In the centre stands a 50m-high (164ft) column erected in memory of the victims of the 1830 and 1848 Revolutions, who were buried beneath the base and whose names are carved on the shaft. The column is surmounted by the gilt winged figure of the Spirit of Liberty by Dumont.

The **Opéra Bastille** was inaugurated for the bicentenary of the 1789 Revolution. Designed by the Canadian architect Carlos Ott, the Opéra National de Paris-Bastille is a harmonious building with a curved façade in several shades of grey that glitters in the sun and gently glows at night. The acoustics of the main auditorium, which can accommodate 2,700 spectators, are superb and the stage is one of the most sophisticated in the world.

Just south of the opera house, a disused railway viaduct has been converted into workshops and showrooms known as the **Viaduc des Arts** illustrating a number of traditional crafts; the Ateliers du Cuivre et de l'Argent (copper and silver workshops) are particularly interesting and there is a small museum.

✚ 123 C8

### Opéra Bastille

✉ Place de la Bastille, 75012 ☎ Recorded information: 01 40 01 19 70 🕐 Listen to the recorded information. Closed Sun ✋ Moderate 🍴 Bar 🚇 Bastille 🚌 20, 29, 65, 69, 76, 86, 87, 91 ❓ Guided tours, shops

### Viaduc des Arts

✉ 9–129 avenue Daumesnil, 75012 🕐 Variable; most workshops open Sun 🍴 Nearby (€) 🚇 Bastille, Ledru-Rollin, Reuilly-Diderot

### BIBLIOTHÈQUE NATIONALE DE FRANCE

Until 1996, the BN, as Parisians call it, was housed in Cardinal Mazarin's former palace situated at the back of the Palais-Royal, extended many times and now stretching from the rue de Richelieu to the rue Vivienne. However, with around 13 million books and as many prints and photographs, it had long been overcrowded. The building of a new library along the river in the 13th *arrondissement* was President Mitterrand's last 'Grand Projet'. The BNF, as it is now called, occupies two sites known as 'Richelieu' and 'François Mitterrand'.

The new library houses the huge stock of printed books and documents and is intended to serve as a public library and a research centre equipped with the most modern means of data transmission. Four corner towers looking like open books surround an imposing base with a central garden where the reading rooms are situated.

The Richelieu building houses manuscripts, prints and medals and holds exhibitions in the Galerie Mansart (Galerie de Photographie), the Galerie Mazarine (which has a magnificent painted ceiling) and the Crypte. The Cabinet des Médailles et des Antiques displays coins and medals from antiquity to the present day as well as objets d'art, cameos and bronzes from the former royal collections.

Two attractive arcades linked to the library, the Galerie Vivienne and the Galerie Colbert, offer an unexpected insight into Parisian social life in the 19th century.

**www.**bnf.fr

➕ 118 E4 ✉ Richelieu: 58 rue de Richelieu, 75002; François Mitterrand: quai François Mauriac, 75013 ☎ Richelieu: 01 53 79 59 59; guided tours: 01 53 79 86 87; François Mitterrand: 01 53 79 59 59 🕓 Richelieu: Galeries and Crypt: Tue–Sat 10–7, Sun 12–7. Cabinet des Médailles: Mon–Sat 1–5, Sun 12–6. François Mitterrand: visits of the building on Tue–Sat 2, Sun 3 by appointment only 💰 Richelieu: moderate; François Mitterrand: free 🍴 Richelieu: restaurant in Galerie Vivienne (€) 🚇 Richelieu: Bourse, Palais-Royal-Musée du Louvre; François Mitterrand: Quai de la Gare 🚌 Richelieu: 29, 39, 48; François Mitterrand: 62, 89

### CARNAVALET, MUSÉE

The Musée Carnavalet traces the history of Paris from antiquity to the present day, and is worth visiting for the building alone. It was once the residence of diarist, Madame de Sévigné, who depicted Parisian society at the time of Louis XIV with great humour. Note the 16th-century lions guarding the entrance and Louis XIV's statue by Coysevox in the centre of the courtyard. In 1989, the museum was linked to the nearby Hôtel Le Peletier de St Fargeau, which dates from the late 17th century. The Hôtel Carnavalet deals with the period from the origins of the city to 1789, with mementoes of Madame de Sévigné and splendid Louis XV

and Louis XVI furniture. The Hôtel Le Peletier de St Fargeau houses collections from 1789 to the present day. The Revolution is extensively illustrated, while the 19th and 20th centuries are represented by a number of reconstructions such as Marcel Proust's bedroom and the art nouveau reception room of the Café de Paris.

✚ 123 B6 ✉ 23 rue de Sévigné, 75003 ☎ 01 44 59 58 58 🕐 Tue–Sun 10–5.40. Closed some public hols ✋ Free, except for some temporary exhibitions 🍴 Restaurants and cafés nearby in rue des Francs-Bourgeois (€–€€€) Ⓜ Saint-Paul 🚌 29, 69, 76, 96 ❓ Guided tours, shops

### CENTRE GEORGES POMPIDOU
See pages 22–23.

### COGNACQ-JAY, MUSÉE
The collections of 18th-century European art bequeathed to the city of Paris by Ernest Cognacq and his wife Louise Jay, founders of the Samaritaine department stores, are displayed in one of the beautiful mansions of Le Marais. The refinement of the Enlightenment period is illustrated by the works of French artists Watteau, Chardin, Fragonard and La Tour, and also by Tiepolo, Guardi and Reynolds. The Rembrandt adds a welcome contrasting note. Various objets d'art, including Saxe and Sèvres porcelain, are exhibited in glass cabinets.

✚ 123 B6 ✉ Hôtel Donon, 8 rue Elzévir, 75003 ☎ 01 40 27 07 21 🕐 Tue–Sun 10–5.40. Closed public hols ✋ Free 🍴 Near by (€–€€) Ⓜ Saint-Paul 🚌 29 ❓ Guided tours, bookshop

## GRANDS BOULEVARDS

These busy arteries, stretching from the place de la République to the Madeleine and lined with cinemas, theatres, cafés and shops, have today fallen victim to their success, choked by traffic jams and disfigured by aggressive neon signs, cheap snack bars and general neglect. The 'boulevards' were laid out as a tree-lined promenade in the 17th century, when some of the city's medieval fortifications were demolished; two ceremonial arches, the Porte St-Martin and the Porte St-Denis, replaced the town gates.

The popularity of the boulevards peaked during the 19th century, with popular attractions in the east (theatre, dancing, circus and busking) and more refined entertainment in the west, especially after the building of the opera house. Several shopping arcades were also opened, including the Passage des Panoramas in boulevard Montmartre, and at the end of the century, one of the first cinemas was inaugurated in boulevard St-Denis by the Lumière brothers.

Today, the boulevards still attract crowds of cinema- and theatregoers but their shabby appearance also encourages a rowdy element, particularly between the Porte St-Martin and the rue de Richelieu. Fortunately, complete renovation is under way.
✚ 118 D4 ✉ From east to west: boulevards St-Martin, St-Denis, de Bonne Nouvelle, Poissonnière, Montmartre, des Italiens, des Capucines and de la Madeleine 🚇 République, Strasbourg-St-Denis, Bonne Nouvelle, Rue Montmartre, Richelieu-Drouot, Opéra, Madeleine

## LES HALLES

Paris's legendary food market has long gone from the centre of the capital, but the name is here to stay, tinged for many Parisians with a certain nostalgia, for when the 19th-century steel-and-glass 'pavillons de Baltard' were removed in 1969 and the noisy activity of the market suddenly stopped, the character of this popular district changed beyond recognition. A vast gaping hole was left between one of the most beautiful churches in Paris and a lovely

Renaissance fountain. A commercial and cultural complex was built underground with a central patio surrounded by glass-roofed galleries that barely reach ground level. Above ground, a garden was laid over the remaining space, with a children's area and shaded walks and more graceful steel-and-glass structures. The underground complex comprises shops, restaurants, a swimming pool, an auditorium, a gymnasium and a tropical greenhouse.

A huge stone head leaning against a hand decorates the semicircular paved area in front of the Église St-Eustache. The latter was built over a period of a hundred years, in a blend of late Gothic, Renaissance and neoclassical styles. From the church, a path leads across the gardens to the square des Innocents and the beautiful Renaissance fountain, built and carved in the mid-16th century by Pierre Lescot and Jean Goujon, who also worked on the Louvre.

✚ 119 F6 ✉ Rue Pierre Lescot, rue Rambuteau, rue Berger, 75001
🍴 In the complex (€) Ⓜ Les Halles 🚌 29, 38, 47

## HÔTEL DE VILLE

The town hall of the city of Paris has been standing on this site since the 14th century. Destroyed by fire during the Paris Commune in 1871, it was rebuilt almost straight away in neo-Renaissance style. On the exterior are 136 statues representing famous historic figures. Nearby stands the 52m-high (170ft) Tour St-Jacques, the only remaining part of a demolished church. In 1648, Pascal used the tower to verify his experiments on the weight of air. Later, a meteorological station was set up at the top and the tower became the property of the city of Paris.

On the east side of the town hall, the Église St-Gervais-St-Protais is a splendid example of a successful blend of Flamboyant Gothic and Classical styles.

✚ 123 B5 ✉ Place de l'Hôtel de Ville, 75004 ☎ 01 42 76 5- 49 🌐 Guided tour by appointment only 🎫 Free Ⓜ Hôtel de Ville 🚌 38, 47, 58, 67, 70, 72, 74, 75, 96

## LE MARAIS

Le Marais, which extends from the Hôtel de Ville to the place de la

Bastille, offers visitors narrow picturesque streets, cafés and bistros, elegant mansions, tiny boutiques and a lively population that includes an important Jewish community. It is also one of the favourite haunts of the gay community.

Around every corner is another delightful mansion. These houses are no longer privately owned: some have been turned into museums, sometimes with striking results (Musée Picasso, ► 87). One of the most imposing, the Hôtel de Soubise, houses the **Musée de l'Histoire de France**, where historic documents are displayed amidst a profusion of Louis XV decoration. An unusual museum dedicated to hunting and nature (**Musée de la Chasse et de la Nature**) is housed in the Hôtel de Guénégaud des Brosses, built by François Mansart (currently closed for restructuring). Here hunting arms dating from prehistory until the 19th century are on display, plus paintings and decorative arts on the subject of hunting.

**Musée de l'Histoire de France**

✚ 123 A6 ✉ Hôtel de Soubise, 60 rue des Francs-Bourgeois, 75003 ☎ 01 40 27 60 96 🌐 Wed–Mon 1.45–5.45 🎫 Inexpensive Ⓜ Hôtel de Ville 🚌 29, 75, 96 ❓ Shop

**Musée de la Chasse et de la Nature**

✚ 123 A6 ✉ Hôtel de Guénégaud des Brosses, 60 rue des Archives, 75003 ☎ 01 53 01 92 40 🌐 Currently undergoing renovation 🎫 Moderate Ⓜ Hôtel de Ville 🚌 29, 75

## PAVILLON DE L'ARSENAL

The late 19th-century iron-and-glass building houses an information centre devoted to Paris's urban planning and architecture throughout its troubled history. The permanent exhibition 'Paris, visite guidée' (Paris, a city in the making) shows the constant evolution of the cityscape by means of a dynamic, chronological display covering the ground, walls and ceiling of the main hall, with models, films and interactive terminals.
**www.**pavillon-arsenal.com

🞧 123 C6 ✉ 21 boulevard Morland, 75004 ☎ 01 42 76 33 97 🕐 Tue–Sat 10.30–6.30, Sun 11–7 ✋ Free 🚇 Sully-Morland 🚌 67, 86, 87

## PÈRE-LACHAISE, CIMETIÈRE DU

The rising ground and abundant vegetation give this cemetery a romantic atmosphere in spite of the great number of unsightly funeral monuments. Many famous people are buried here, including Chopin, Molière, Oscar Wilde, Delacroix, Balzac, even the unhappy lovers Héloïse and Abélard. One of the most visited graves is that of Jim Morrison, lead singer of The Doors. In the southeast corner stands the Mur des Fédérés where the last 'communards' were shot in 1871.

✚ 119 E8 (off map) ✉ Boulevard de Ménilmontant, 75020 ☎ 01 55 25 82 10 🕐 Mon–Fri 8–6, Sat 8.30–6, Sun 9–6 (5.30 in winter) 🖑 Free ⓜ Père-Lachaise ❓ Guided tours (in English) Sat 3 in summer

## PICASSO, MUSÉE

The Picasso collection was brought together after the artist's

death and consists of works donated to the State by his family in lieu of death duties, and his private collection – together totalling more than 200 paintings, sculptures, prints, drawings and ceramics. The Hôtel Salé, at the heart of the historic Marais, was chosen to house this important collection. Like many other mansions in the area, it had been neglected and underwent extensive renovation to turn it into a museum. The interior decoration is very discreet, focusing attention on the beautiful stone staircase with its elegant wrought-iron banister.

Displayed in chronological order, the works illustrate the different phases of Picasso's artistic creation and the various techniques he used, from the blue period tainted with a certain pessimism

(*Autoportrait bleu*), through the more optimistic pink period, to the successive Cubist periods. The tour of the museum is a fascinating journey in the company of one of the most forceful creative minds of this century. Picasso's private collection includes works by Renoir, Cézanne, Rousseau, Braque and others.
**www.**musee-picasso.fr

✚ 123 A6 ✉ Hôtel Salé, 5 rue de Thorigny, 75003 ☎ 01 42 71 25 21 🕐 Apr–Sep Wed–Mon 9.30–6; Oct–Mar Wed–Mon 5.30. Closed 1 Jan, 25 Dec 🖑 Moderate ⓜ St-Paul, Saint-Sébastien Froissart, Chemin Vert 🚌 29, 69, 75, 96 ❓ Guided tours, shop

## VOSGES, PLACE DES

This is Paris's oldest square and perhaps the loveliest for its moderate size, its discreet charm, its delightful brick-and-stone architecture and its peaceful central garden. We owe this brilliant piece of town planning to 'Good King Henri' (Henri IV) whose initiative launched the development of Le Marais. The square is lined with identical pavilions over continuous arcading, dormer windows breaking up the monotony of the dark slate roofs; in the centre of the south and north sides stand two higher pavilions, known respectively as the Pavillon du Roi and

Pavillon de la Reine. The square changed names during the Revolution and was finally called 'place des Vosges' in 1800 in honour of the first *département* to pay its taxes!

Number 6, where Victor Hugo (1805–85) lived for 16 years, is now a museum (**Maison de Victor Hugo**), containing family mementoes, furniture, portraits, drawings by the writer himself as well as reconstructions of the various homes Hugo lived in.

✚ 123 B7 ✉ 75004 🚇 St-Paul, Bastille, Chemin Vert 🚌 20, 65, 69, 76

**Maison de Victor Hugo**

✉ 6 place des Vosges, 75004 ☎ 01 42 72 10 16 🕐 Tue–Sun 10–5.40. Closed public hols 💷 Free 🍴 Restaurants nearby 🚇 Bastille 🚌 69, 76 ↔ Musée Carnavalet, place de la Bastille

# Montmartre

**This unassuming village overlooking Paris became a myth during the 19th century, when it was taken over by artists and writers attracted by its picturesque surroundings and bohemian way of life. La 'Butte' (the mound) managed to retain its village atmosphere and now that the area has become a major tourist attraction, an undefinable nostalgia lingers on, perpetuating Montmartre's magic appeal.**

In its heyday, the district was the favourite haunt and home of many famous artists. They met in cafés and in cabarets such as the Moulin-Rouge (1889), whose singers and dancers acquired world-wide fame through Toulouse-Lautrec's paintings and posters. Today it is a mix of teeming tourist traps such as place du Tertre and Sacre-Coeur, and quiet cobbled enclaves, with whitewashed cottages and more than a hint of its former 'village' atmosphere.

## AU LAPIN AGILE

At the corner of rue St-Vincent, look for the Montmartre vineyard and the Au Lapin Agile nightclub. Renowned as the rendezvous of young artists and writers in the early 1900s, the club is still popular, its cabaret combining popular music with sharp-edged repartee.
www.au-lapin-agile.com

✚ 124 B3 ✉ 22 rue des Saules, 75018 ☎ 01 46 06 85 87 ⊕ Tue–Sun 9.15pm–2am ✋ Expensive (includes a drink) 🚇 Lamarck-Caulaincourt

## BATEAU-LAVOIR

Halfway up the hill of Montmartre, a wooden construction known as the Bateau-Lavoir, where, among others, Picasso, Braque and Juan Gris had their studios, was the modest birthplace of Cubism. Destroyed by fire in 1970, it has since been rebuilt.

✚ 124 C2 ✉ 13 place Emile-Goudeau, 75018 🚇 Abbesses

## ESPACE MONTMARTRE SALVADOR DALÍ

With more than 300 works by Salvador Dalí (1904–89) on display, including sculptures, illustrations, lithographs and some of his less familiar paintings, this is the biggest Dalí collection in France.

✚ 124 C3 ✉ 9–11 rue Poulbot, 75018 ☎ 01 42 64 40 10 ⊕ Daily 10–6 ✋ Moderate 🚇 Abbesses

## LA VILLETTE

See pages 40–41.

## MARCHÉ AUX PUCES DE ST-OUEN

This is reputedly the largest flea market in the world, covering 7ha (17 acres) just north of Montmartre. More than 2,000 stalls are grouped into 13 different *marchés*, each with its own specialities, from bric-à-brac to pricey antiques. Be prepared to haggle, pay in cash and keep watch out for pickpockets.

✚ 124 A4 (off map) ✉ Streets around rue des Rosiers, 75018 ⊕ Sat–Mon 9.30–6 (some stands open earlier) 🚇 Porte de Clignancourt, Garibaldi

## MONTMARTRE, CIMETIÈRE DE

Montmartre's cemetery is the most famous graveyard in Paris after Père-Lachaise (➤ 86–87). It is filled with the graves of the famous, such as composers Hector Berlioz and Jacques Offenbach, artists Edgar Degas and Jean Honoré Fragonard, writers Heinrich Heine and Émile Zola (whose remains were removed to the Panthéon), and film director François Truffaut. You can pick up a plan of the graves at the main entrance, and there are also guided tours at certain times.

➕ 124 C1 ✉ 20 avenue Rachel, 75018 ☎ 01 53 42 36 30 🕐 Mid-Mar to early Nov Mon–Fri 8–6, Sat 8.30–6, Sun 9–6; early Nov to mid-Mar Mon–Fri 8–5.30, Sat 8.30–5.30, Sun 9–5.30 (last entry 15 mins before closing)
🚇 Place de Clichy/Blanche

## MOULIN DE LA GALETTE

The Moulin de la Galette, one of
Montmartre's two remaining windmills
was the venue for a popular ball
that inspired Renoir's famous painting:
*Le Bal du Moulin de la Galette*, now in
the Musée d'Orsay (➤ 34–35). Built
in 1622, the 'Biscuit Windmill' was
named after the delicious galette
biscuits made here using flour from the mill.

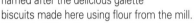 124 C2 ✉ Rue Tholozé, 75018 (privately owned) Ⓜ Abbesses

## MOULIN-ROUGE

In its heyday, the district was the favourite haunt and home of
many famous artists. They met in cafés and in cabarets such as
the Moulin-Rouge ('Red Windmill'), whose singers and dancers
acquired world-wide fame through Toulouse-Lautrec's paintings
and posters. It was never actually a windmill but was launched as a
cabaret venue in 1889. Shows, with the trademark displays of the
can-can, are still performed here today, but at a price.
www.moulinrouge.fr

124 D2 ✉ 82 boulevard de Clichy, 75018 ☎ 01 53 09 82 82
⊙ Spectacles nightly at 9 and 11. Combined dinner and show at 7pm
Expensive Ⓜ Blanche

## MUSIQUE, MUSÉE DE LA

Housed within the vast Cité de la Musique (➤ 41), the museum
presents a permanent exhibition consisting of some 900 musical
instruments dating from the Renaissance to the present day, as
well as works of art and objets d'art inspired in some way by
music. Regular concerts and lectures and various cultural events
take place in the 230-seat auditorium.

124 D4 (off map) ✉ 221 avenue Jean-Jaurès, 75019 ☎ 01 44 84 44 84
⊙ Tue–Sat 12–6, Sun 10–6 Moderate Ⓜ Porte de Pantin 🚌 75, 151, PC

## SACRÉ-COEUR, BASILIQUE DU

The white domes and campaniles of this neo-Byzantine basilica stand out against the skyline, high above the rooftops of the capital. Its construction at the top of Montmartre was undertaken as a sign of national reconciliation and hope after the bitter defeat suffered by France in the 1870 war against Prussia. Funds were raised by public subscription and work started in 1875, but the basilica took nearly 45 years to build and was inaugurated only in 1919, at the end of another war!

The view over Paris from the terrace in front of the building is breathtaking; an impressive number of steps leads down to the place St-Pierre; from the dome, an even more stunning panoramic view stretches for 50km (31 miles) around the city. The interior of the basilica is profusely decorated with mosaics.

**www**.sacre-coeur-montmartre.com

➕ 124 C3 ✉ Place du Parvis du Sacré-Coeur, 75018 ☎ 01 53 41 89 00 🕐 Basilica: daily 6am–11pm; dome and crypt: daily 9–6 (7 in summer) 💳 Basilica: free; dome and crypt: inexpensive 🚇 Abbesses (from here walk along rue Yvonne Le Tac, then take funicular or walk up steps) 🚌 30, 31, 80, 85, Montmartrobus ❓ Shops

## ST-PIERRE, ÉGLISE

Just to the west of Sacré-Coeur is the diminutive 12th-century church of St-Pierre-de-Montmartre, consecrated in 1147 and one of Paris's oldest churches. This lovely, peaceful church is all that remains of the Benedictine abbey of Montmartre.

➕ 124 C3 ✉ 2 rue du Mont-Cenis, 75018 🚇 Abbesses

## TERTRE, PLACE DU

The whole of place du Tertre (*tertre* means hillock), one of the most hectic tourist spots in Paris, is filled with easels and would-be artists, all trying to sell their work or sketch you. (Note, you are not obliged to pay if they produce an unsolicited portrait of you.) For most of the year it bustles with crowds who come to eat and people-watch in this tiny, café-bordered square at the heart of Montmartre, but during winter, it manages to retain its rural atmosphere.

At No 6, on one corner of the square, you will find La Mère Catherine (☎ 01 46 06 32 69), an unassuming little bistro dating from the Napoleonic era and very popular with the Russian troops who occupied the city in 1814. They were in the habit of banging the table and shouting 'bistro!' (meaning 'quick!') which gave rise to the name for such unpretentious eating places. Here you can occasionally sample Montmartre's own wine made with grapes from the area's one surviving vineyard.

✚ 124 C3 ✉ Place du Tertre, 75018 🚇 Abbesses

## VIEUX MONTMARTRE, MUSÉE DE

The Musée de Vieux Montmartre has works and memorabilia by the artists who lived here, and the narrow cobbled streets of the 'Butte' still have some amazing sights to offer, including a vineyard in the picturesque rue des Saules and two windmills in the twisting rue Lepic.

✚ 124 C3 ✉ 12 rue Cortot, 75018 🕐 Tue–Sun 11–6. Closed 1 Jan, 1 May, 25 Dec ✋ Inexpensive 🚇 Lamarck-Caulaincourt 🏪 Exhibitions, bookshop

# Excursions

'Île de France', as the Paris region is called, means the heart of France; and this is exactly what it has always been and still is, the very core of the country, a prosperous and dynamic region, inhabited by one French person in five, with Paris in its centre. Roads, motorways and international railway lines converge on this central region, which has become one of Europe's main crossroads, with two major international airports.

Besides its tremendous vitality, the Île de France offers visitors attractive natural assets, a rich cultural heritage and a gentle way of life. The countryside is domestic rather than spectacular, graced by picturesque villages, country inns, manor houses, historic castles, abbeys, cathedrals and beautiful parks and gardens.

## CHANTILLY, CHÂTEAU DE

The Château de Chantilly houses the Musée Condé, named after one of its most distinguished owners, Le Grand Condé. The 16th-century Petit Château contains the 'Princes' apartments' and a library full of precious illuminated manuscripts, including the 15th-century *Les Très Riches Heures du Duc de Berry*; the Grand Château, destroyed during the Revolution and rebuilt in Renaissance style at the end of the 19th century, houses a magnificent collection of paintings by Raphael, Clouet, Ingres, Corot and Delacroix, as well as porcelain and jewellery.

Facing the famous racecourse, the 18th-century stables have been turned into the Musée Vivant du Cheval, illustrating the various crafts, jobs and sports connected with horses.

**www.**chateaudechantilly.com

✚ 125 B2 ✉ 40km (25 miles) north of Paris. BP 70243, 60631 Chantilly Cedex ☎ Château and Musée Conde: 03 44 62 62 62; Musée Vivant du Cheval: 03 44 57 40 40 🕐 Chateau: Mar–Oct Wed–Mon 10–6, Nov–Feb Wed–Mon 10.30–12.45, 2–5. Musée du Cheval: Mar–Oct daily 10.30–6.30; Nov–Feb daily 2–6 ✋ Moderate 🍴 Near the station (€) 🚃 Gare du Nord to Chantilly-Gouvieux

## DISNEYLAND® RESORT PARIS

Disneyland® Resort Paris offers fantasy, humour, *joie de vivre*, excitement and the latest technological devices to ensure that your visit is a memorable one. Besides Disneyland® Park and Walt Disney Studios® Park, there is a whole range of 'typically' American hotels to tempt you to stay on for a day or two.

**www.**disneylandparis.com

✚ 125 C3 ✉ 30km (19 miles) east of Paris. BP100 77777 Marne-la-Vallée ☎ UK: 08705 03 03 03; in France: 01 60 30 60 30 🕐 Varies with the season ✋ Moderate 🍴 Inside the park (€–€€€) 🚃 RER A Marne-la-Vallée/Chessy

### FONTAINEBLEAU, CHÂTEAU DE

A fountain or spring, now in the Jardin Anglais, is at the origin of this splendid royal residence, which started out as a hunting pavilion at the heart of a vast forest. It was François I who made Fontainebleau into the beautiful palace it is today, although it was later remodelled by successive monarchs. The imposing horseshoe staircase decorating the main façade was the scene of Napoleon I's moving farewell to his faithful

guard in 1814. Beyond this building lies the Etang des Carpes (carp pool) with a lovely pavilion in its centre, and further on the formal French gardens. The oldest part of the palace, including the keep of the medieval castle, surrounds the Cour Ovale. The State Apartments contain paintings, furniture and objets d'art, the fine coffered ceiling of the Salle de Bal and frescoes in the Galerie François I.

✚ 125 D3 ✉ 65km (40 miles) southeast of Paris. 77300 Fontainebleau ☎ 60 71 50 70 ◷ Wed–Sun 9.30–12.30, 2–5 (reduced hours Sep–Jun). Closed 1 Jan, 1 May, 25 Dec ♨ Moderate ⅰ In the town nearby (€–€€€) ⊚ Gare de Lyon to Fontainebleau-Avon and ▯ A or B ? Guided tour, shops

### FRANCE MINIATURE

This open-air museum comprises a huge three-dimensional map of France on which 166 miniature historic monuments have been arranged. There are models of the Tour Eiffel, Sacré Coeur, Mont-St-Michel, the pont du Gard and Gallo-Roman arenas, as well as many beautiful castles, all made to a scale of 1:30. Here and there, a typical French village focuses on ordinary daily life.

✚ 125 C1 ✉ 25km (15 miles) west of Paris. 25 route du Mesnil, 78990 Elancourt ☎ 01 30 62 40 78 ◷ Apr–early Nov 10–6 (7 in Jul and Aug); last admission 1 hour before closing ♨ Moderate ⅰ Two restaurants (€–€€) ⊚ Gare Montparnasse ? Audiovisual show, outdoor activities

## PARC ASTÉRIX

This theme park is based on the comic adventures of a friendly little Gaul named Astérix and his companions, who are determined to resist the Roman invaders. The story became famous world-wide through a series of strip cartoons by Goscinny and Uderzo, which have since been translated into many languages.

Inside the park, visitors are invited to share Astérix's adventures as they wander through the Gauls' Village, the Roman City and Ancient Greece, travel on the impressive roller-coaster of the Great Lake and journey back and forth in time along the rue de Paris!

➕ 125 B3 ✉ 30km (19 miles) north of Paris. BP 8, 60128 Plailly ☎ 03 44 62 34 04 🕐 Early Apr–early Sep 9.30 or 10–6 or 7. Closed some days outside peak season of mid-Jun to Aug ✋ Moderate 🍴 Several choices (€–€€) 🚇 RER B3 from Châtelet or Gare du Nord to Roissy-Charles-de-Gaulle 1 then G Courriers Île-de-France every half hour ❓ Gift shops, picnic areas, pushchair (stroller) rental

## SAINT-CLOUD, PARC DE

This beautiful park, on the outskirts of Paris, extends over a vast hilly area overlooking the Seine. The castle designed by Jules-Hardouin Mansart for Louis XIV's brother, was destroyed by fire in 1870 and razed to the ground in 1891. It had been Bonaparte's favourite official residence when he was consul of the Republic.

The park was designed by Le Nôtre. At the top the site of the former castle is now a terrace offering lovely views of the capital. Nearby is the Jardin du Trocadéro, an English-style garden with an ornamental pool and an aviary. There are many shaded alleyways offering delightful walks through the 460ha (1,136-acre) park.

✉ 125 C2 ✉ 11km (7 miles) west of Paris. 92210 Saint-Cloud ☎ 01 41 12 02 90 🕐 Daily 7.30am–8.50pm (7.50pm Nov–Feb, 9.50 May–Aug) ✋ Free 🍴 Cafés (€) 🚇 Pont de Saint-Cloud

## SAINT-GERMAIN-EN-LAYE

The historic city of Saint-Germain-en-Laye clusters round its royal castle, once the favourite residence of Louis XIV. François I commissioned the present Château Vieux (Old Castle) and retained Saint-Louis's chapel and the 14th-century square keep, now surmounted by a campanile. Le Nôtre later designed the gardens and the magnificent 2,400m-long (7,872ft) Grande Terrasse. The Sun King stayed in Saint-Germain for many years and during that time private mansions were built around the castle for members of his court. When the court moved to Versailles in 1682, the castle was somewhat neglected but it was eventually restored by Napoleon III and turned into the Musée des Antiquités Nationales, which houses interesting archaeological collections illustrating life in France from earliest times to the Middle Ages.

✚ 125 C2 ✉ 23km (14 miles) west of Paris.

### Château de Saint-Germain-en-Laye

✉ BP 3030, 78105 Saint-Germain-en-Laye Cedex ☎ 01 39 10 13 00 🕐 Wed–Mon 9–5.15. Closed some public hols ✋ Inexpensive 🚇 RER Saint-Germain-en-Laye ❓ Guided tours, shops

## VAUX-LE-VICOMTE, CHÂTEAU DE

This architectural gem cost its owner, Nicolas Fouquet, his freedom and eventually his life. Fouquet had commissioned the best artists of his time: Le Vau for the building, Le Brun for the decoration and Le Nôtre for the gardens. Louis XIV was invited to a reception given for the inauguration of the castle in 1661. He did not take kindly to being outshone: Fouquet was arrested and spent the rest of his life in prison, while Louis commissioned the same artists to build him an even more splendid castle, Versailles.

The castle stands on a terrace overlooking magnificent gardens featuring canals, pools and fountains.

✉ 125 D3 ✉ 51km (32 miles) southeast of Paris. Domaine de Vaux-le-Vicomte, 77950 Maincy ☎ 01 64 14 41 90 🕐 Late Mar to mid-Nov Mon–Fri 10–1, 2–6, Sat, Sun 10–6. Candlelit visits: early May to mid-Oct Sat 8pm–midnight (also Fri Jul–Aug) 🖐 Expensive 🚉 Gare de Lyon to Melun then taxi

## VERSAILLES, CHÂTEAU DE

The physical expression of a king's superego, Versailles turned out to be one of the most splendid castles in the world through the genius of the artists who built and decorated it. What began as a modest hunting lodge became the seat of government and political centre of France for over a hundred years. A town grew up around the castle to accommodate the court. Several thousand men worked on the castle for 50 years, thousands of trees were transplanted, and 3,000 people could live in it.

The castle is huge (680m/2,230ft long) and it is impossible to see everything in the course of one visit. Aim for the first floor where the State Apartments are, including the famous Galerie des Glaces, as well as the Official Apartments and the Private

Apartments of the royal couple, situated on either side of the marble courtyard. The north wing contains the two-floor Chapelle St-Louis built by Mansart and the Opéra, added later, by Gabriel.

The focal point of the park is the Bassin d'Apollon, a magnificent ornamental pool with a bronze sculpture in its centre representing Apollo's chariot coming out of the water. Two smaller castles, Le Grand Trianon and Le Petit Trianon, are also worth a visit, and Le Hameau, Marie-Antoinette's retreat, offers a delightful contrast.

**www.**chateauversailles.fr

✉ 125 C2 ✉ 20km (12.5 miles) southwest of Paris. 78000 Versailles ☎ 01 30 83 78 00 🕐 Château: Tue–Sun 9–5.30 (6.30 in summer); closed some public hols. Trianons: daily noon–5.30 (6.30 in summer). Parc: daily 7–5.30 (up to 9.30pm depending on season; from 8am winter) ceremonies ♿ Moderate 🍴 Cafeteria (€) and restaurant (€€) 🚆 Gare St-Lazare to Versailles Rive Droite

# in and around the Forêt de Fontainebleau

**The forest of Fontainebleau extends over a vast area along the left bank of the Seine, to the southeast of the capital.**

*Start at the Porte d'Orléans and follow the A6 motorway towards Evry and Lyon. Leave at the Fontainebleau exit and continue on the N37 for 7km (4 miles); turn right to Barbizon.*

This village gave its name to a group of landscape painters who settled there in the mid-19th century. They were joined later by some of the future Impressionists: Renoir, Sisley and Monet. The **Auberge Ganne**, which they decorated with their paintings, is now a museum.

*Leave Barbizon towards Fontainebleau.*

Take time to visit the château (➤ 102), or at least the park, and to stroll around the town.

*Drive southeast along the D58 , bearing left at the Y-junction. Turn right onto the Route Ronde (D301).*

This scenic route takes you through the forest and offers many possibilities for walking and cycling.

*Turn left on the D409 to Milly-la-Forêt.*

This small town nestling round an imposing covered market is a traditional centre for growing medicinal plants. The Cyclop (1km/0.5 miles north) is a monumental modern sculpture which took 20 years to complete.

*Take the D372 for 3.5km (2 miles); bear left for Courances.*

The **Château de Courances** looks delightful, set like a jewel in a magnificent park designed by Le Nôtre, with pools, canals and small waterfalls.

*Return to the main road and continue for 5km (3 miles), then rejoin the motorway back to Paris.*

**Distance** 143km (89 miles)
**Time** 7–9 hours depending on length of visits
**Start/end point** Porte d'Orléans
**Lunch** Le Caveau des Ducs ✉ 24 rue de Ferrare, 77300 Fontainebleau ☎ 01 64 22 05 05

**Auberge Ganne**
✉ 92 Grande Rue, 77630 Barbizon ☎ 01 60 66 22 27 🕔 Apr–Sep Wed–Mon 10–12.30, 2–5 🖐 Moderate

**Château de Courances**
✉ 91240 Milly-la-Forêt ☎ 01 40 62 07 71 🕔 Apr–Oct Sat, Sun and public hols 2–6.30 🖐 Moderate ❓ Guided tours

### VINCENNES, CHÂTEAU DE

This austere castle, situated on the eastern outskirts of Paris, was a royal residence from the Middle Ages to the mid-17th century. Inside the defensive wall, there are in fact two castles: the 50m-high (164ft) keep (currently undergoing repair) built in the 14th century, which later held political prisoners, philosophers, soldiers, ministers and churchmen; and the two classical pavilions built by Le Vau for Cardinal Mazarin in 1652, Le Pavillon de la Reine, where Anne d'Autriche, mother of Louis XIV lived, and Le Pavillon du Roi, where Mazarin died in 1661. The Chapelle Royale, started by Saint-Louis and completed by François I, stands in the main courtyard.

✉ 125 C2 ✉ 6km (4 miles) east of Paris. Avenue de Paris, 94300 Vincennes
☎ 01 48 08 31 20 🕓 Daily 10–noon, 1.15–5 (6 in summer). Closed 1 Jan, 1 May, 1 Nov, 11 Nov, 25 Dec 💰 Inexpensive 🚇 Métro: Château de Vincennes
❓ Guided tours, shops

# Index

# Acknowledgements

The Automobile Association would like to thank the following photographers, companies and picture libraries for their assistance in the preparation of this book.

Abbreviations for the picture credits are as follows – (t) top; (b) bottom; (c) centre; (l) left; (r) right; (AA) AA World Travel Library.

**4l** Metro, AA/C Sawyer;  **4c** Louvre, AA/J Tims;  **4r** Lafeyette shopping bag, AA/C Sawyer; **5l** Château de Fontainbleau, AA/M Jourdan; **5c** Eiffel Tower, AA/B Rieger; **5r** La Coupole, AA/B Rieger; **6/7** Metro, AA/C Sawyer; **10** Jazz musicians, Digitalvision; **12** Charles de Gaulle aiport, AA/C Sawyer; **12/13** Gare du Nord, AA/C Sawyer; **14** RER sign, AA/C Sawyer; **15** Bus, AA/M Jourdan; **16** Phone box, AA/K Paterson; **20/21** Louvre, AA/J Tims; **22** Centre Georges Pompidou, AA/W Voysey; **23t** Sculpture, Centre Georges Pompidou, AA/T Souter; **23b** View from Centre Georges Pompidou, AA/J Tims; **24t** Champs Elysées sign, AA/P Kenward; **24c** Arc de Triomphe, AA/P Enticknap; **24b** Parc Monceau, AA/K Paterson; **24/25** Arc de Triomphe, AA/M Jourdan; **26** La Grande Arche de la Défence, AA/J Tims; **26/27** La Grande Arche de la Défense, AA/T Souter; **27** La Grande Arche de la Défense, AA/T Souter; **28** Dome, Les Invalides, AA/J Tims; **28/29** Les Invalides, AA/K Paterson; **29** Église du Dôme, Les Invalides, AA/K Paterson; **30/31** Le Louvre, AA/M Jourdan; **32t** Candles, Notre-Dame, AA/C Sawyer; **32b** Notre-Dame, AA/C Sawyer; **32/33** Notre-Dame, AA/C Sawyer; **33** View of Notre-Dame, AA/T Souter; **34t** Musée d'Orsay, AA/M Jourdan; **34b** Musée d'Orsay, AA/M Jourdan; **34/35** Musée d'Orsay, AA/P Enticknap; **35** Musée d'Orsay, AA/M Jourdan; **36** Couple, river Seine, AA/M Jourdan; **36/37** River Seine, AA/C Sawyer; **38** Eiffel Tower, AA/P Enticknap; **38/39** Eiffel Tower, AA/J Tims; **40/41** Parc de la Villette, AA/M Jourdan; **41t** Parc de la Villette, AA/M Jourdan; **41b** Parc de la Villette, AA/M Jourdan; **42/43** Lafeyette shopping bag, AA/C Sawyer; **45** Café, AA/K Paterson; **46/47t** Salle de Gens, AA/K Paterson; **46/47b** Pont Neuf, AA/T Souter; **48** Institut du Monde Arabe, AA/C Sawyer; **49** Institut du Monde Arabe, AA/M Jourdan; **50t** Musée de Cluny, AA/K Paterson; **50b** Carved heads, AA/J Tims; **50/51** Panthéon, AA/J Tims; **52** Jardin des Plantes, AA/T Souter; **53** Sainte-Chapelle, AA/J Tims; **54** River Seine, AA/M Jourdan; **55** Shakespeare & Company, AA/K Paterson; **56/57** Musée National Eugène Delacroix, AA/J Tims; **59** Institut de France, AA/P Kenward; **60** Jardin du Luxembourg, AA/M Jourdan; **60/61** Street scene, Montparnasse, AA/M Jourdan; **62** Rodin's *The Thinker*, AA/M Jourdan; **64** St-Sulpice church, AA/M Jourdan; **66** Arc de Triomphe, AA/M Jourdan; **69** Fountain, Place de la Concorde; AA/B Rieger; **70** Lavin shop window, AA/C Sawyer; **71** Grand Palais, AA/M Jourdan; **72** Musée Jacquemart-André, AA/P Kenward; **73** Musée Marmottan-Monet, AA/J Tims; **74** Musée Nissim de Camondo, AA/J Tims; **75** Courtyard, Palais-Royal, AA/M Jourdan; **76** Jardin des Tuileries, AA/M Jourdan; **77** Antique market, AA/K Paterson; **78/79** Opéra Bastille, AA/C Sawyer; **80/81** Musée Carnavalet, AA/K Paterson; **82/83t** Église St-Eustache, AA/J Tims; **82/83b** Les Halles, AA/M Jourdan; **84/85t** Rue des Francs-Bourgeois, AA/C Sawyer; **84/85b** Hôtel de Ville, AA/M Jourdan; **86** Cimetière du Père-Lachaise, AA/M Jourdan; **87** Musée Picasso, AA/M Jourdan; **88t** Café, AA/B Rieger; **88b** Place des Vosages, AA/K Paterson; **89** Street artist, Montmartre, AA/M Jourdan; **90/91** Marché Aux Puces de St-Ouen, AA/C Sawyer; **92/93** Cimetière de Montmartre, AA/P Kenward; **93** Moulin de la Galette, AA/J Tims; **94/95** Sacré-Coeur, AA/J Tims; **96** Place du Tertre, AA/T Souter; **97** Poster, AA/T Souter; **98/99** Château de Fontainbleau, AA/M Jourdan; **101** Château de Chantilly, AA/D Noble; **102** Château de Fontainbleau, AA/D Noble; **102/103** Parc Astérix, Parc Asterix; **103/104** Château de Vaux-le-Vicomte, AA/B Rieger; **106/107** Château de Versailles, AA/M Jourdan; **107t** Château de Versailles, AA/M Jourdan; **107b** Château de Versailles, AA/D Noble; **108** Gorges de Franchard, AA/D Noble; **110** Château de Vincennes, AA/J Tims; **111** Les Deux Magots, AA/M Jourdan.

Every effort has been made to trace the copyright holders, and we apologise in advance for any accidental errors. We would be happy to apply the corrections in the following edition of this publication.

# Maps

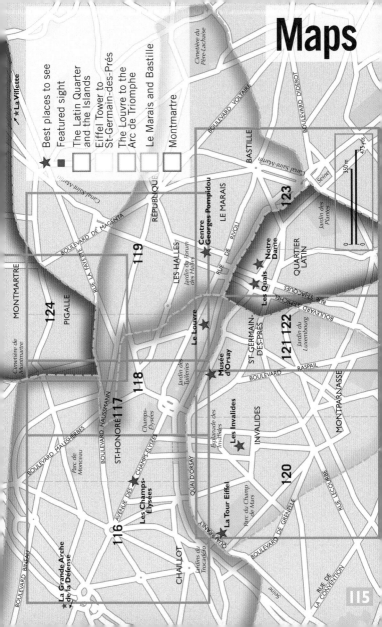

**Best places to see**

★ Featured sight
■ Featured sight

☐ The Latin Quarter and the Islands
☐ Eiffel Tower to St-Germain-des-Prés
☐ The Louvre to the Arc de Triomphe
☐ Le Marais and Bastille
☐ Montmartre

★ La Villette

Cimetière du Père-Lachaise

Cimetière de Montmartre

MONTMARTRE

124

PIGALLE

BOULEVARD DE MAGENTA

RUE LA FAYETTE

BOULEVARD HAUSSMANN

BOULEVARD MALESHERBES

Parc de Monceau

ST-HONORÉ

117

118

119

RÉPUBLIQUE

LES HALLES

Jardin du forum des Halles

Canal Saint-Martin

BOULEVARD VOLTAIRE

BASTILLE

Canal Saint-Martin

Centre Georges-Pompidou ★

LE MARAIS

RUE DE RIVOLI

123

Seine

Jardin des Plantes

BOULEVARD DIDEROT

350 m
475 yds

Notre Dame ★

Les Quais ★

QUARTIER LATIN

RUE ST-JACQUES

BOULEVARD ST-MICHEL

ST-GERMAIN-DES-PRÉS

121-122

Jardin du Luxembourg

BOULEVARD RASPAIL

MONTPARNASSE

Le Louvre ★

Jardin des Tuileries

Musée d'Orsay ★

BOULEVARD

116

AVENUE DES CHAMPS-ELYSÉES

Les Champs-Elysées ★

Champs-Elysées

QUAI D'ORSAY

Esplanade des Invalides

Les Invalides ★

INVALIDES

120

La Tour Eiffel ★

Parc du Champ de Mars

QUAI BRANLY

Jardins du Trocadéro

CHAILLOT

La Grande Arche de la Défense ★

BOULEVARD BINEAU

Seine

BOULEVARD DE GRENELLE

RUE LECOURBE

RUE DE LA CONVENTION

115

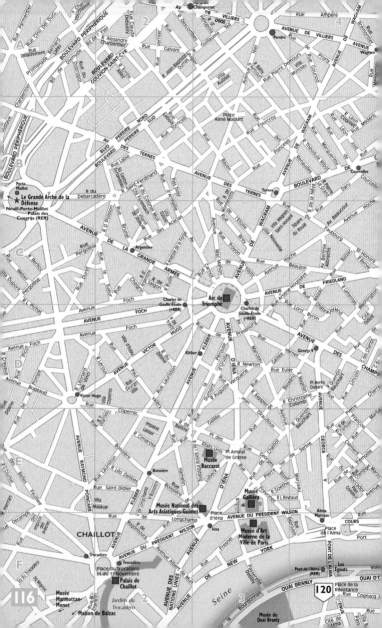

A
B
C
D
E
F

1 2 3 4

AV de Champerret
VILLIERS
R Claude
RUE
Ampère
RUE
R Descombes
Guillaume
D908
BOULEVARD PÉRIPHÉRIQUE
Char
R Cino del Duca
Promenade
R Delaizement
Bernard
BOULEVARD
GOUVION-SAINT-CYR
Pereire
AVENUE DE VILLIERS
AVENUE
Wagram
R Alexandre
Charpentier
R Jean Baptiste
Galvani
Villa
Aublet
Place
Aimé Maillart
RUE
RUE
Rue Fourcroy
RUE
Rue Léon
R Léon Cogniet
Médéric
BOULEVARD
Ternes
BOULEVARD
DE
Courcelles
Courcelles
AVENUE
DES
TERNES
R de la Néva
Porte
Maillot
Le Grande Arche de la
Défense
Neuilly-Porte-Maillot
Palais des
Congrès (RER)
R du
Debarcadère
AVENUE
DE LA
GRANDE
Argentine
ARMÉE
AVENUE
DE
FRIEDLAND
Arc de
Triomphe
Charles de
Gaulle-Étoile
(+RER)
Charles de
Gaulle-Étoile
(+RER)
AVENUE
DES
CHAMPS
FOCH
AVENUE
D'IÉNA
AVENUE
Kléber
George V
AVENUE
VICTOR
HUGO
Victor Hugo
Rue Euler
Pl Henry
Duhant
GEORGE
AVENUE
RAYMOND
Boissière
Boissière
Rue Saint-Didier
AVENUE
D'IÉNA
POINCARÉ
Musée
Baccarat
Pl Amiral
de Grasse
V
KLÉBER
Musée National des
Arts Asiatiques-Guimet
Place
d'Iéna
Iéna
Musée
Galliéra
AVENUE DU PRÉSIDENT WILSON
Alma-
Marceau
Place
de l'Alma
Musée d'Art
Moderne de la
Ville de Paris
COURS
PONT DE L'ALMA
CHAILLOT
Trocadéro
AVENUE DU
PRÉSIDENT WILSON
AVENUE
DES
NATIONS UNIES
AVENUE
DE
NEW
YORK
Pont de l'Alma
(RER)
Les
Egouts
Place de la
Résistance
QUAI D'O
Place du Trocadéro
et du 11 Novembre
Palais de Chaillot
Cognacq...
116
Musée
Marmottan-
Monet
Maison de Balzac
Jardins du
Trocadéro
2
Seine
3
Passerelle
Debilly
QUAI BRANLY
Musée du
Quai Branly
120

120

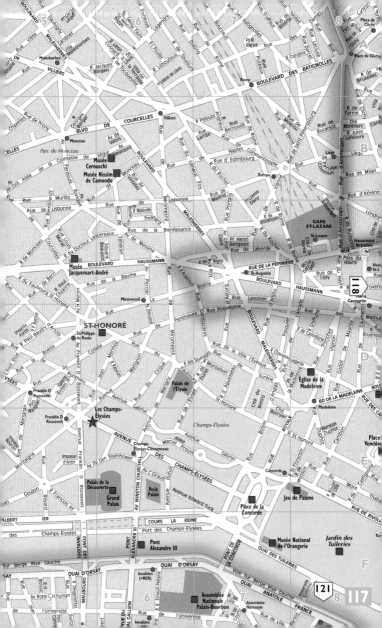

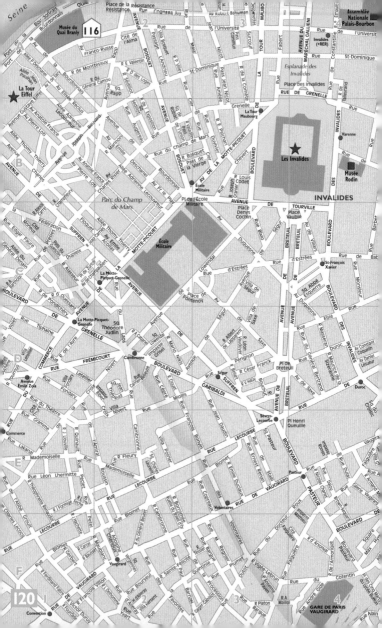

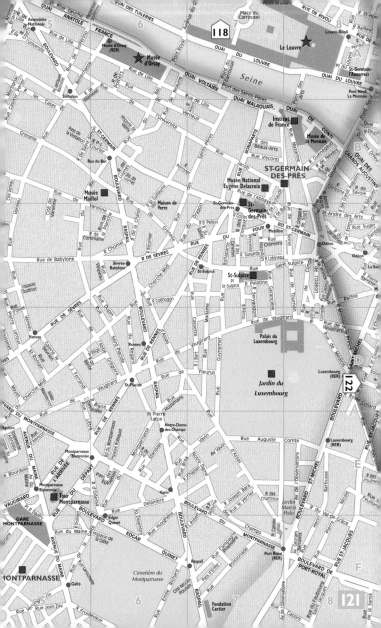

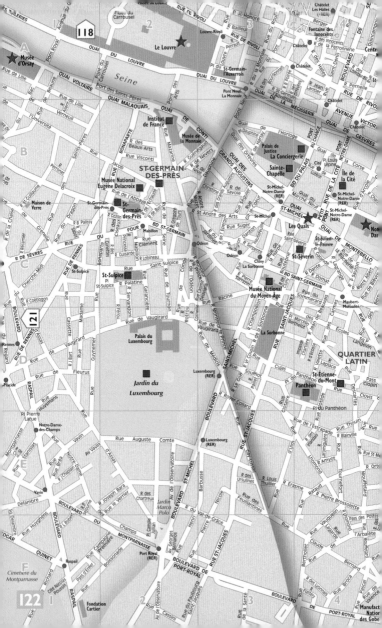

A TUILERIES

Place du Carrousel

118

2

Le Louvre ★

ST-Honoré

R. Bailleul

RUE DE RIVOLI

Louvre-Rivoli

Châtelet

Fontaine des
Innocents

4

Les Halles

Berger

R. Berger

R. de la Ferronnerie

Centre

★ Musée
d'Orsay

QUAI    DU    LOUVRE

Seine

QUAI VOLTAIRE

QUAI MALAQUAIS

Pont Neuf
La Monnaie

QUAI DE LA MÉGISSERIE

AVENUE VICTOR

RUE DE RIVOLI

B

Institut
de France

Musée de
la Monnaie

ST-GERMAIN-
DES-PRÈS

Palais de
Justice
La Conciergerie

Sainte-
Chapelle

Île de
la Cité

RUE DE GESVRES

Notre-Dame

Musée National
Eugène Delacroix

St-Germain-
des-Prés

BD ST-GERMAIN

St-André des Arts

Rue Suger

ST-MICHEL

Les Quais

St-Julien-
le-Pauvre

Nôtre Dame ★

C

FOUR

Odéon

Odéon

St-Séverin

St-Sulpice

Pl
St-Sulpice

BD SAINT-GERMAIN

Musée National
du Moyen-Âge

121

RUE DE RENNES

RUE DE VAUGIRARD

La Sorbonne

QUARTIER
LATIN

D

Palais du
Luxembourg

Luxembourg
(RER)

St-Etienne-
du-Mont

Panthéon

Jardin du
Luxembourg

BOULEVARD

Pl Pierre
Latue

Notre-Dame-
des-Champs

RUE AUGUSTE COMTE

Luxembourg
(RER)

E

Vavin

Jardin
Marco
Polo

BOULEVARD    DE    PORT-ROYAL

F

BOULEVARD

MONTPARNASSE

Port Royal
(RER)

BOULEVARD DE
PORT-ROYAL

Cimetière du
Montparnasse

122

Fondation
Cartier

Manufact
Nation
des Gobe

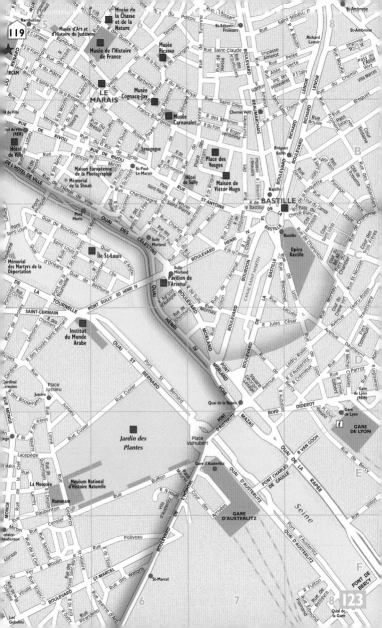

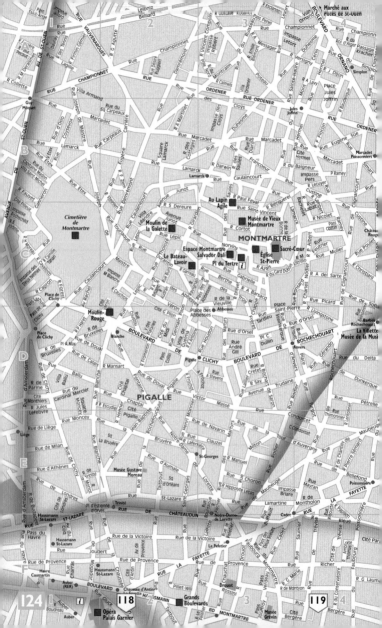

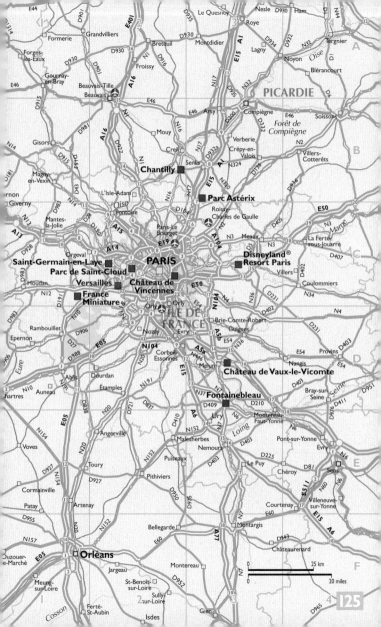

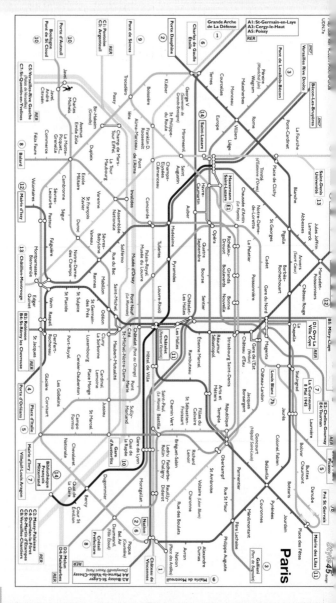

Paris

Sky 45